Metaphysics
and the Modern World

Metaphysics and the Modern World

Donald Phillip Verene

CASCADE *Books* · Eugene, Oregon

Cascade Books
An Imprint of Wipf and Stock Publishers
199 W. 8th Ave., Suite 3
Eugene, OR 97401

www.wipfandstock.com

PAPERBACK ISBN: 978-1-4982-3801-4
HARDCOVER ISBN: 978-1-4982-3803-8
EBOOK ISBN: 978-1-4982-3802-1

Cataloguing-in-Publication data:

Verene, Donald Phillip, 1937–
Metaphysics and the modern world / Donald Phillip Verene.
Description: Eugene, OR : Cascade Books, 2016 | Includes bibliographical references and index.
Identifiers: ISBN 978-1-4982-3801-4 (paperback) | ISBN 978-1-4982-3803-8 (hardcover) | ISBN 978-1-4982-3802-1 (ebook)
Subjects: LCSH: Metaphysics. | Civilization, Modern.
Classification: BD125 .V47 2016 (print) | BD125 .V47 (ebook)

Manufactured in the U.S.A.   AUGUST 26, 2016

Metaphysics is the finding of bad reasons
For what we believe upon instinct, but
To find these reasons is no less an instinct.

—F. H. BRADLEY, *APPEARANCE AND REALITY*

Contents

Preface

ARISTOTLE'S WORK KNOWN AS the *Metaphysics* begins with the claim that all human beings (*anthrōpoi*) by nature desire to know. It is reflected in the Latin phrase *homo sapiens*, those beings capable of *sapientia* or wisdom. To know is to know something in particular, but to know in the greatest sense is to know the causes of things and how all things comprise a whole. "The wise man," Aristotle says, "knows all things, as far as possible, although he has not knowledge of each of them in detail." He says, further, that "knowing all things must belong to him who has in the highest degree universal knowledge; for he knows in a sense all the instances that fall under the universal" (982a). Philosophy, as its name asserts, is not the love of knowledge but the love of wisdom. Wisdom is held by both the Greeks and the Latins to be the knowledge of things divine and human and acquaintance with the causes of each.

The cause of the love of wisdom itself is wonder (*thauma*), according to Aristotle: "For it is owing to their wonder that men both now begin and at first began to philosophize." This wonder that initiates the pursuit of wisdom is the result of thought leading itself to a point of impasse, an *aporia*, a difficulty sufficient to show us that we are ignorant of the actual cause or nature of something. As Aristotle says, "A man who is puzzled and wonders thinks himself ignorant (whence even the lover of myth is in a sense a lover of wisdom, for myth is composed of wonders)" (982b). The lover of myth finds the object of wonder in the image, in which the immediacy of perception is preserved. In myth the *aporia* is overcome through the power of metaphor to portray the similar in the dissimilar. The mythic grasp of the object is an extension of perception, which forms the world through the senses, through their power to present objects to thought. Like perception itself, mythical thought makes no distinction between truth and error.

Every metaphor is a fable in brief. The mythic, the fabulous, can be narrated over and over, a twice-told tale, giving an imaginative order to experience.

In the *Poetics*, Aristotle says, "The greatest thing by far is to be a master of metaphor. It is the one thing that cannot be learnt from others; and it is also a sign of genius" (1459a). The wonders of which myth is composed are the beginnings of thought. Each myth is a true story, a *vera narratio*. The myth is the original form of the complete speech, the speech that puts the whole into words. Mythical thought, or the form of thought before logical thought, is not governed by the principle of non-contradiction. The diversities of the world are simply tied together in the power of the mythic narrative. Mythic thought moves from one thing to another, not in an effort to seek a single cause but to invest any single event with multiple causes, thus increasing its reality by making it more vivid. The event's liveliness is enhanced for the mythic mind; the more the causes associated with the event are in opposition to each other, the more the event is a *coincidentia oppositorum*, and the richness of its reality is increased.

Once thought gains internal distance from the immediacy of the mythic narrative as the form of experience, thought can never truly return to this immediacy. It can no more do this than an adult can properly be a child again. The mythic world passes into memory, and becomes the basis of imagination. All that "seems" in the mythic world also equally "is." The wonder that originates metaphysics occurs when a distinction is apprehended between "seems" and "is." What "is" takes on the status of a thing-in-itself, our apprehension of it being its manner of appearance. Metaphysics becomes myth remembered. Metaphysics becomes the art of attempting, in conceptual terms, to remake the whole that is first realized in the myth. To do this is an impossible task because the two terms of this separation from which the *aporia* of metaphysical thought arises can never be reduced to each other. What the mythic narrative naturally achieved remains, for rational discourse, always just out of reach.

As the American poet Carl Sandburg says in his little treatise *Incidentals*, "Truth consists of paradoxes and a paradox is two facts that stand on opposite hilltops and across the intervening valley call each other liars." Metaphysical thought, like philosophy itself, is a process of doubling up. Where myth can at its best produce coincidence, metaphysics can at its best produce dialectic. Metaphysics must find a way to distinguish truth from error and, in so doing, find a way to make this distinction a truth.

The two dominant movements of modern philosophy are the analytic and hermeneutical schools. Both are the offspring of the problem of knowledge. Neither employs contemplation. Both are dedicated to the belief that language can literally state the truth. The tropes of metaphor and irony are to be set aside as the medium of literature. Both of these schools are versions of dead-serious thinking. In this pursuit, both aim to make philosophy respectable. To accomplish this aim the Socratic search for self-knowledge and the questions Socrates asks must be set aside.

Analytic philosophy is not a unified position in the sense of a single subject matter or a single method, variously applied. It is a style, an attitude of mind governed by the view that philosophy is intellectual problem-solving. Philosophers are to seek out puzzles and seek solutions to them by means of the precise use of language, logical operations, and scientifically supported conclusions. The puzzles can be taken from any of the traditional fields of philosophical thought, including ethics and even aesthetics. It is philosophy piecemeal, often to be done in article form in professional journals, always cast in terms of arguments. What puzzles are taken as important is a matter of convention. One has only to seek out articles from many years ago, for example, on the verification principle, to grasp the fashionable component of analytic philosophy. To read such articles is to read yesterday's philosophical newspapers. For the analytic philosopher, the history of philosophy is either of little interest or stands as a warehouse of past arguments and puzzles, some of which might be ordered up and reconstituted.

Hermeneutic philosophy puts the "text" in the place of the puzzle. Once hermeneutical exposition is divorced from its original sense of bringing forth the meaning of sacred texts whose truth and significance are given, the hermeneutical philosopher faces the problem of which texts are worth exposition. One can only fall back on tradition. Texts that tradition has identified as of interest become the subject of hermeneutical activity. In order to be not simply looking backward, and tied to existing texts, some hermeneutical philosophy employs the text as a metaphor, such that any social, political, historical, legal, or cultural institution can be considered a text and its meaning brought forth in discursive language. The abiding problem hermeneutical philosophy faces is epistemic relativism—which texts are worth hermeneutical analysis. Meaning is not truth, and truth found here or there is not the True. The problem for hermeneutical philosophy is the whole, the formulation of the complete speech, the presentation of all that there is.

Overlooked by the commitment to the problem of knowledge is dialectic, the power of thought to double up. As Aristotle says, a double is not two separate things, or it would not be a double. A double is one thing in two guises of itself: "But surely to be double and to be 2 are not the same; if they are, one thing will be many" (*Metaph.* 987a). The problem of knowledge seeks to see the truth of the object only once, and to see all else as error. Metaphysics seeks to see the object twice, as it seems and as it is. This double-sightedness means that to say what a thing is, is to say what it is and to say what it is not.

Metaphysical thought requires what James Joyce in *Finnegans Wake* called "two thinks at a time" and a "twone." The only way thought can confront *aporiai* is by grasping both sides of the difficulty at once as aspects of itself. This double grasping forces thought from simply reflecting on its object as an other and thus finds the object as an other within itself. In this manner we pass from the reflective holding of the object at a distance to the speculative seeing into its "inner form." Wisdom, which philosophy loves, requires us to think something twice, to think it as it is and as it is not. What is, then, is a twice-told tale, a double truth, in which the one-sidedness of the mentality of the problem of knowledge is overcome.

R. G. Collingwood, in beginning his *Essay on Metaphysics*, says, "In writing about metaphysics it is only decent, and it is certainly wise, to begin with Aristotle." And on this advice I have begun. The chapters that follow are both a work of metaphysics and at the same time a work on metaphysics. I make no attempt to separate specific metaphysical questions from the question of what metaphysics is. Metaphysics as a field of philosophy is philosophy at its limits. Philosophy can go no further. Metaphysics as philosophy at its limits is a point captured in the coining of the term "metaphysics," when the ancient editor of Aristotle's works, Andronicus of Rhodes, called that which came after the *Physics*, *meta ta physika* ("after the things of nature").

As Simplicius held, *meta* may be interpreted as "beyond" as well as "after." Metaphysics may best be understood by Aristotle's own term of "first philosophy" or "first science" (1026a16). Physics or natural science is "second philosophy," for it, like mathematics, is connected to matter, as one kind of matter is perceptible and there is another that is intelligible. Metaphysics treats that which is "separable [from matter] and immovable"

(1037a). Furthermore, "There is a science which investigates being as being and the attributes which belong to this in virtue of its own nature. Now this is not the same as any of the so-called special sciences; for none of these others deals generally with being as being" (1003a). In the beginning of the *Metaphysics*, Aristotle calls this science of being or first philosophy *sophia*, or wisdom itself. This wisdom is composed of *epistemē* as a knowledge of the causes of being; it is the highest kind of *epistemē*.

Metaphysics has as its subject matter those great questions about the nature of things, including human nature, that remain after the pursuit of those questions that can be treated by specific lines of inquiry and investigation. Metaphysics is rooted in the human phenomenon of speculative thinking. Every human being whose mental life turns in upon itself encounters questions regarding the divine, the natural, and the human. For many, such questions arise and are a cause for wonder. But they are then put aside in one of two ways. Either some answer is decided upon and only later found to be questionable, or they are put aside as unanswerable and unimportant, an unnecessary annoyance, only to reappear, to be re-examined, and again to be put aside. But for a few, such questions cease to remain in the background of mental life; they are brought forward as themes of thought.

Once these few have given themselves over to these themes, they find themselves in some sense in the position described by Plato in the myth of the cave, regarding the former prisoner who has returned, having glimpsed the sun: "And before his eyes had recovered—and the adjustment would not be quick—while his vision was still dim, if he had to compete again with the perpetual prisoners in recognizing the shadows, wouldn't he invite ridicule? Wouldn't it be said of him that he'd returned from his upward journey with his eyes ruined and that it isn't worthwhile even to try to travel upward?" (*Rep.* 517a).

Would they not also, perhaps, find themselves in the position described by Spinoza, in the first pages of his essay "On the Improvement of the Understanding," when he says, "Further reflection convinced me, that if I could really get to the root of the matter I should be leaving certain evils for a certain good. I thus perceived that I was in a state of great peril, and I compelled myself to seek with all my strength for a remedy, however uncertain it might be; as a sick man struggling with a deadly disease, when he sees that death will surely be upon him unless a remedy be found, is compelled to seek such a remedy with all his strength, inasmuch as his whole hope lies therein." Even further, would they not find themselves in agreement with Berkeley's line, in his preface to his *Three Dialogues between Hylas and Philonous*: "We spend our lives in doubting of those things which other men evidently know and believing those things which they laugh at and despise"?

Finally, might they, in their attempt to resolve the connection between the world of appearance and the world of reality and discover the really real, find themselves in Hegel's inverted world (*verkehrte Welt*) of the third chapter of his *Phenomenology of Spirit*, so that "what is *like* in the first world is *unlike* to itself, and what is *unlike* in the first world is equally *unlike to itself*, or it becomes *like* to itself. Expressed in determinate moments, this means that what in the law of the first world is sweet, in this inverted in-itself is sour, what in the former is black is, in the other, white. What in the law of the first is the north pole of the magnet is, in its other, supersensible in-itself [viz. in the earth], the south pole; but what is there south pole is here north pole" (PS 158; 122). Our thought is led into a nightmare from which we are trying to awake.

Finding ourselves in the position these passages describe, we may be led to ask ourselves, as Socrates does in the *Phaedrus*, when he contemplates whether he knows himself, as the Delphic oracle has instructed, "Am I a beast more complicated and savage than Typhon, or am I a tamer, simpler animal with a share in a divine and gentle nature?" (230a).

Despite the labyrinth into which thought and the mind's eye are led, the object that metaphysics seeks remains. As Aristotle puts it, this object is "being *qua* being" (*to on he on*), which is different from the being of individual beings (*onta*). The nature of individual beings can be the subject of the particular sciences, but the nature of Being (*on*) is "one" (*hen*) and it is the subject of metaphysics. Our initial state of ignorance, produced by the *aporiai* that thought encounters and that lead to wonder, places us in a position as if we were tied up "and it is not possible to untie a knot which one does not know. But the difficulty in our thinking points to a knot in the object; for in so far as our thought is in difficulties, it is in like case with those who are tied up; for in either case it is impossible to go forward" (995a). These difficulties can be resolved only by *diaporia*, an exploration of the various routes that have been taken by others. This exploration requires a dialectical process of considering the views of those who have faced the difficulties of metaphysical thought before us.

In the chapters that follow I shall chart a course through the history of philosophy, selecting certain figures as guides in the development of metaphysical ideas. In so doing I shall keep in mind that metaphysics is for most persons the most opaque of all the fields of philosophical inquiry. Traveling this route will offer a concrete apprehension of how the question of what metaphysics is may be answered. Metaphysics will be seen as part of human culture, as a human endeavor to approach the ultimate and to think the most universal of thoughts. My aim is more the essay than the treatise. It is to suggest the courses thought may take. My purpose is that recommended by Horace, when he proposes that what is said should instruct, delight, and move (A.P. 333). If something of this ideal is accomplished regarding the contents advanced herein, my purpose shall be served. Philosophy, once conducted as a lively act within the agora of Athens, can now best be conducted within the agora of history, the Republic of Letters. In so doing we may capture some degree of contemplation, of *theōria*, of which Aristotle speaks in the *Nicomachean Ethics*, and from this standpoint think dialectically, as do Hegel and some of those after him.

Chapter 1 considers the conditions in mythical and primal religious thought, from which metaphysics is born. Chapter 2 examines the nature of the medieval ontological argument, not as such known to the ancients, but which initiates the very basis of subsequent metaphysical thought. Chapter 3 analyzes the principle of *coincidentia oppositorum* as put forth in the works of the Renaissance founders of modern metaphysics, Nicholas of Cusa and Giordano Bruno. Chapter 4 presents Giambattista Vico's metaphysics of history as based on providence. Chapter 5 examines the conception of the "true infinity" that G. W. F. Hegel regards as the most important problem in philosophy. Chapter 6 formulates the dialectic of spirit (*Geist*) and life that Ernst Cassirer advances as underlying his philosophy of symbolic forms. Chapter 7 describes the cosmology of "actual entities" that A. N. Whitehead projects from the standpoint of modern physics and which he connects to a philosophical theology as the "final interpretation" of the nature of things. These chapters are not intended as historical discussions but as extractions and developments of the systematic views embodied in the metaphysics of each of these figures. They are my four masters of modern metaphysics.

In progressing through this pattern of development, in the attempt to grasp the idea of the ultimate, of being *qua* being, we might do well to keep before us the lines of two poets. The first is Dante, who in the beginning of the *Divine Comedy* glimpses "the delectable mountain, the source and cause of every happiness" (1.78). But his way to climb this *dilettoso monte* is threatened by the "dark wood," the *selva oscura* of error in which he finds himself, and by the beasts he encounters—the leopard (*lonza*) of malice and fraud, the lion (*leone*) of violence and ambition, and the she-wolf (*lupa*) of incontinence. The glimpse of the little hill or Mount of Joy causes him to pursue its truth by another route, with Virgil, the symbol of human reason. In metaphysics, a project of human reason, we are pulled on by wonder, a glimpse of the possibility of something ultimate, beyond the *aporiai*, generated by reflective rather than speculative thought.

The second poet is Schiller, from whose poem "Friendship" ("Die Freundschaft") Hegel glosses the lines with which he ends his *Phenomenology of Spirit*. It portrays the problem of the relation of God to the world, in which the divine is left with its own infinity as companion.

> Friendless was the great World Master,
> Felt a lack—thus he created spirits,
> > Blessed mirror of his bliss!—
> Still found the highest being no likeness
> From out of the chalice of the whole realm of the soul
> > Foams for Him—infinity.

The spirits (*Geister*) are true infinity that, taken together, provide a glimpse of the ultimate being or *Weltenmeister*, whose actions are present in the providence of the world order. Only through the "cunning of Reason" (*List der Vernunft*) can we glimpse this divine order in things. Once seen, it is to metaphysics we must turn to comprehend it as a work of reason.

In calling attention to these poets as a beginning point, I am following Vico's advice, in a criticism he makes of Descartes for beginning philosophy from rational doubt, and of Locke for beginning it from the senses. Vico says, "The metaphysics of the philosophers must agree with the metaphysic of the poets, on this most important point, that from the idea of a divinity have come all the sciences that have enriched the world with all the arts of humanity" (NS 1212).

Metaphysics must take its beginning from the beginning of culture— the world as originally made, through the mythopoeic formation of feeling and imagination that is later reformed by the power of reason. The first human thought is of the ultimate, the divine presence, and by naming it, the power of the name allows all in the world to be named, from which comes knowledge and, later, wisdom, when reason joins the diverse things into a whole, expressed by a complete speech. How this can be comprehended is the first subject to which I wish to turn.

No book is the work of a single author. It requires the presence of friends. I wish to thank my colleagues at Emory and other universities who generously became the first readers of this work: Thora Ilin Bayer, Ann Hartle, George Benjamin Kleindorfer, Donald Livingston, David Lovekin, and Frederick Marcus. With their thoughts, like so many other times, they have been indispensable to my efforts. I greatly thank Molly Black Verene, not only for transferring my handwritten text into typescript, but for her many editorial skills and helpful suggestions.

Abbreviations and Citations

Plato   *Complete Works*. Edited by John M. Cooper. Indianapolis: Hackett, 1997. Cited by the standard "Stephanus numbers."

Aristotle   *The Complete Works: Revised Oxford Translation*. Edited by Jonathan Barnes. 2 vols. Princeton: Princeton University Press, 1984. Cited by the standard notation to Bekker's edition of the Greek text.

Classics   References to works of Greek and Latin classical literature are to the volumes of the Loeb Classical Library, Harvard University Press, using standard forms of citation, with wording of quotations occasionally modified.

Vico   *The New Science of Giambattista Vico*. Translated by Thomas Goddard Bergin and Max Harold Fisch. Ithaca: Cornell University Press, 1984. Italian edition: *Opere*. Edited by Andrea Battistini. 2 vols. Milan: Mondadori, 1990. Cited by NS plus the paragraph enumeration common to both editions.

Hegel   *Phenomenology of Spirit*. Translated by A. V. Miller. New York: Oxford University Press, 1977. German edition: *Phänomenologie des Geistes*. Edited by Johannes Hoffmeister. 6th ed. Hamburg: Meiner, 1952. Cited by PS plus the paragraph enumeration of the English edition, followed by the page number of the German edition.

     The Science of Logic. Translated by George di Giovanni. Cambridge: Cambridge University Press, 2010. German edition: *Wissenschaft der Logik*. Edited by Georg Lasson. 2 vols. Hamburg: Meiner, 1971. Cited by SL plus the page number of the English edition, followed by the page number of the German edition.

Cassirer   *The Philosophy of Symbolic Forms*, vol. 4, *The Metaphysics of Symbolic Forms*. Edited by John Michael Krois and Donald Phillip Verene. Translated by John Michael Krois. New Haven: Yale University Press, 1996. German edition: *Zur Metaphysik der symbolischen Formen*, vol. 1 of *Nachgelassene Manuskripte und Texte*. Edited by John Michael Krois and Oswald Schwemmer. Hamburg: Meiner, 1995. Cited by PSF 4 plus the page number of the English edition, followed by the page number of the German edition.

The Philosophy of Symbolic Forms, vol. 1, *Mythical Thought*; vol. 2, *Language*; vol. 3, *The Phenomenology of Knowledge*. Translated by Ralph Manheim. New Haven: Yale University Press, 1953–57. Cited by PSF plus the volume and page number of the English edition, followed by the page number of the German edition. *Gesammelte Werke*, vols. 11–13. Meiner: Hamburg, 2001–2.

Whitehead   *Process and Reality: An Essay in Cosmology*. New York: Macmillan, 1929. Cited by PR, followed by the page number.

Adventures of Ideas. New York: Macmillan, 1933. Cited by AI, followed by the page number.

Introduction: Myth and Metaphysics

Two Ways of Knowing: *Narratio* and *Ratio*

THERE ARE TWO WAYS to discover what a thing is. We can attempt to discover its beginning and from this *principium* recover its genesis and development. In this way we determine its nature by answering the questions of from when and where. The thing, then, is a matter of recollection. In his little treatise *On Memory*, Aristotle says, "When one wishes to recollect, that is what he will do: he will try to obtain a beginning of movement whose sequel shall be the movement which he desires to reawaken. This explains why attempts at recollection succeed soonest and best when they start from a beginning" (451b). By applying memory as recollection to a thing, the thing also enters the imagination. As Aristotle says, "If asked, of which among the parts of the soul memory is a function, we reply: manifestly of that part to which imagination [*phantasia*] also appertains; and all objects of which there is imagination are in themselves objects of memory" (450a). The image generated in the imagination by memory allows us to see the nature of the thing with our mind's eye. We are able to make the thing a subject of narration.

A second way is to attempt to delineate the properties of a thing, to understand it conceptually as a matter of logical reflection, description, and analysis. If we approach metaphysics in this way, we may say that it is a division of philosophy that considers questions of the nature of being and the cosmos and in so doing treats of the relations that obtain between reality and appearance. Metaphysics is a wider investigation than that carried on in the particular sciences because it traditionally considers the existence of non-physical entities, such as the existence or non-existence of God. Metaphysics further differs from the particular sciences in that they proceed on the basis of assumptions that metaphysics can make explicit and subject to rational scrutiny. Although, as we shall see, all thought may be regarded as implicitly involving metaphysical claims, including all philosophical thought, some philosophers are explicitly committed to metaphysics. These are most of the great figures in the history of philosophy, among whom are Plato, Aristotle, Anselm, Aquinas, Cusanus, Bruno, Descartes, Spinoza, Vico, and Hegel, with Cassirer and Whitehead representing two recent views.

Seen from this perspective, metaphysics can be conceived as treating a list of problems regarding substance, object, subject, event, cause, existence, self, God, and so forth. Textbooks on metaphysics often have chapters on each, approaching them as problems on which there are varying and controversial views. The approach I wish to take is the first—the recollective—for it is in the narrative grasp of beginnings and development that the problems of the list arise and confront us. If we see metaphysics as a panorama of arguments and counterarguments our thought can go nowhere. Such an oscillation of *sic et non* is ultimately boring, even though the arguments may initially engage us. Metaphysics is rightfully reduced, as Kant has shown, to antinomies, paralogisms, and the difficulties of the ontological argument. For any argument it is never beyond human wit to devise a counterargument, given sufficient latitude and time. Kant is also correct in his observation that metaphysical thought is a propensity of mind. It cannot be eliminated from human nature. Let us, then, look at metaphysics as an intellectual art, a necessary part of the human propensity toward contemplation.

Metaphysics is grounded in the phenomenon of speculation, the attempt to think and portray the order and nature of things as a whole. The whole, as Vico says, is "really the flower of wisdom,"[1] and, as Hegel adds in his famous sentence, "The true is the whole" (*das Whare ist das Ganze* [PS 20; 21]). Metaphysics is the heart of philosophy, the attempt to make the love (*philia*) of wisdom (*sophia*) in speech (*logos*). It can do us no harm to listen to these metaphysical speeches that follow, and in fact, if we do, it is likely "we shall fare well," as Plato says.

---

1. Vico, *Study Methods*, 77.

In working our way through such speeches we may take the position that they are part of *philosophia perennis*, each presenting a partial truth of the whole, none individually (nor all taken together) silencing the human project of speculation, and none a final, complete speech making any further philosophizing unnecessary. This approach is more rewarding than the unrelenting enactment of the *ars critica* of attempting to assert one system as final and finished, or simply placing one system against another, seeing nothing but differences. Metaphysical disputation, although intellectual exercise, yields little, because argument never rises to the level of wisdom. Metaphysics is an affair purely of reason connected to experience; it does not have the power of experiment and evidence available to the progress of the particular sciences.

Those attracted to metaphysics would do well to consider the claim in "The Earliest System-Program of German Idealism" to which Hegel subscribed: "The philosopher must possess just as much aesthetic power as the poet. Men without aesthetic sense are our literal-minded philosophers [*unsere Buchstabenphilosophen*]. The philosophy of spirit is an aesthetic philosophy. One can in no way be ingenious [*geistreich*], one cannot even argue [*raisonnieren*] about history ingeniously [*geistreich*] without aesthetic sense."[2] It is ideas, not simply arguments that take us to a formulation of the whole. In holding these views I do not intend to be an enemy of argument but stand with Socrates, in the *Phaedo*, that despite the limits of argument, argument is natural and proper to philosophical exchange and we should not be misologists (89d).

Without metaphysics, philosophy rapidly devolves into philosophizing that is nothing more than social opinion, pseudo social science, or ideology. To turn philosophy into a reflection on politics, as is frequently done today, is to abandon philosophy's origin as the love of wisdom. Metaphysics is the fountain from which true philosophizing flows. Unless thought is taken to its limits, what the philosopher says has no ground in the nature of things and is a form of journalism and opinion.

Pythagoras and Socrates

If metaphysics is the highest field of philosophy, or perhaps the science of being, ontology, that lies within it, we would do well to recall the famous scene in which Pythagoras is said to have coined the word *philosophos*. It

2. Hegel, "System-Programme," 511.

is related by Heraclides of Pontus, a man of letters and member of Plato's Academy, in his dialogue *Peri tēs apnou*, or "The case of the woman whose breathing had stopped," a medical work in which scientific and miraculous elements are combined, of which only fragments remain. It concerns the apotheosis of Empedocles. In the midst of the consideration of this issue, and extolling Empedocles's success in resuscitating the woman, the episode of the coining of *philosophos* is described.[3]

One of the likely purposes of Heraclides' dialogue was to dispel the claim that Empedocles, in an attempt to join the pantheon of gods, died by hurling himself into the volcano on Etna. The conditions of his death and apotheosis are tied to a feast that honored his success in reviving the woman from her coma. On this account, Empedocles did not depart with the others from the banquet but remained, and during the night he disappeared. His disappearance was termed a miracle—that he had been called to the heavens by a mighty voice and a light shining in the sky.

Empedocles was able to resurrect the unconscious woman, when all physicians had failed, because he considered the one factor they had neglected: the state of her soul. The soul of the woman had been separated from her body, and she was brought back to life by its recall. The physicians were doctors of the body, but Empedocles was a doctor of the soul. He succeeded because he had a knowledge of human nature as a whole. The need of this knowledge for the proper practice of medicine is made clear in the *Phaedrus*, in which Socrates asks Phaedrus, "Do you think, then, that it is possible to reach a serious understanding of the nature of the soul without understanding the nature of the world as a whole?" Phaedrus replies, "Well, if we're to listen to Hippocrates, Asclepius' descendant, we won't even understand the body if we don't follow that method" (270b). Thus a knowledge of the whole is required in treating any aspect of the human condition. The true physician must not only be skilled in medicine, he must also be wise, since "wisdom is a knowledge of things divine and human and the causes of each," as mentioned above. Socrates says, then, that "proceeding by any other method would be like walking with the blind" (270d).

The love of wisdom is what makes the philosopher a doctor of the soul. Thus we are led, in Heraclides' dialogue, to recall the origin of the name and nature of philosophy, which occurs in an exchange between Pythagoras and Leon, the tyrant of Phlius. The fullest account of this conversation comes to us in the last book of Cicero's *Tusculan Disputations*, the

---

3. Gottschalk, *Heraclides*, chap. 2.

account of which is attributed to Heraclides (5.3). It is worth our while to consider this famous statement at length. Cicero writes, "And though we see that philosophy is a fact of great antiquity, yet its name is, we admit, of recent origin. For who can deny that wisdom itself at any rate is not only ancient in fact but in name as well? And by its discovery of things divine and human, as well as the beginnings and causes of every phenomenon, it gained its glorious name with the ancients." Wisdom is knowledge raised to the level of the whole or of all that exists—all things divine and human, known in terms of their beginnings and ends.

Those who are thought to possess wisdom, Cicero says, include the Seven Sages of ancient Greece and the Homeric mythological personages of Lycurgus, Ulysses, and Nestor, who are engaged in human endeavors, and Atlas, Prometheus, and Cepheus, whose actions connect them to the heavens and the gods. "And with these began the succession of all those who devoted themselves to the contemplation of nature and were both held to be and named wise men, and this title of theirs penetrated to the time of Pythagoras who, according to Heraclides of Pontus, the pupil of Plato and a learned man of the first rank, came, the story goes, to Phlius and with a wealth of learning discussed certain subjects with Leon the ruler of the Phliasians." This succession of wise men or *sophoi* are those figures we categorize as the Presocratics, beginning with Thales of Miletus, who is also counted among the Seven Sages. Although these thinkers make pronouncements about the nature of the soul or *psychē*, the object of their thought is to contemplate nature as a whole in terms of the one in the many. The soul-principle, for example, is extended by Anaximenes to the universe at large.

Cicero continues: "And Leon after wondering at his talent and eloquence asked [Pythagoras] to name the art in which he put most reliance; but Pythagoras said that for his part he had no acquaintance with any art, but was a philosopher." In this moment *philosophos* is coined by modifying the Greek for *sophos*, one who is wise, with *philos*, one who loves, one who has a strong attraction to or affinity for. In so doing, Pythagoras makes a new subject matter for thought, *philosophia*, by uniting the idea of friendly love (*philia*) with wisdom (*sophia*). This subject matter is not a particular art to be practiced among other arts. It is a unique way of thinking in universal terms about the whole. It is an ultimate sense of knowing. But Pythagoras does not claim to possess this sense of wisdom. He is only attracted to it as one is attracted in a friendship. Pythagoras's answer is clever in the greatest sense, because the subtext of his answer is that only the gods are wise, in the sense of what is ultimate and beyond the human. Were Pythagoras to claim that he is truly wise in this ultimate art of knowing, he would have a power beyond that of the tyrant Leon, who has complete political power.

Pythagoras's answer to Leon establishes the distinction between the philosopher and the city that is to be the theme of Platonic-Socratic philosophy. His answer awards this new being dignity, but at the same time appears to render this new subject harmless to the *polis*. This special position of the *philosophos* is made clear in Pythagoras's description of the nature of this human type in his further answer to Leon: "Leon was astonished at the novelty of the term and asked who philosophers were and in what they differed from the rest of the world. Pythagoras, the story continues, replied that the life of man seemed to him to resemble the festival [at Olympia] which was celebrated with most magnificent games before a concourse collected from the whole of Greece; for at this festival some men whose bodies had been trained sought to win the glorious distinction of a crown, others were attracted by the prospect of making gain by buying or selling, whilst there was on the other hand a certain class, and that quite the best type of free-born men, who looked neither for applause or gain, but came for the sake of the spectacle and closely watched what was done and how it was done."

The love of wisdom is seen as entailing a particular kind of life. To attach oneself to the pursuit of wisdom is to approach the world in a particular way. This ancient notion of philosophy as a kind of human existence stands in contrast to the modern conception of philosophy as a field of knowledge that requires no particular type of life, such that the philosopher can pass quite unnoticed, engaged in ordinary social interchange. This sense of the philosopher is established by Descartes, in which philosophy is pursued alone, in the study, and the philosopher, in the same manner as the scientist, emerges simply to announce the results of the research done. The attitude of mind the philosopher requires to produce such results is generally not made public. Modern philosophy seeks to be respectable. Ancient philosophy does not, as Socrates attempts to explain in the *Crito*. Pythagoras fled Croton just ahead of its citizens. Socrates refused to leave Athens and accepted his death penalty. Plato leaves Syracuse in fear of his life, on his third visit. Even Aristotle leaves Athens lest the Athenians disgrace themselves twice in regard to philosophy. Boethius writes his

Consolation of Philosophy, which was to become the most widely read work of the Middle Ages, while awaiting his death, in prison, in Rome.

Cicero concludes his account: "So also we, as though we had come from some city to a kind of crowded festival, leaving in like fashion another life and nature of being, entered upon this life, and some were slaves of ambition, some of money; there were a special few who, counting all else as nothing, closely scanned the nature of things; these men gave themselves the name lovers of wisdom (for that is the meaning of the word philosopher); and just as at the games the men of truest breeding looked on without any self-seeking, so in life the contemplation and discovery of nature far surpassed all other pursuits."

To the kinds of lives the ancients acknowledge—that of the many, not mentioned but implied here, which is the pursuit of pleasure; and that of the few, the pursuit of honor, and also wealth, which is tied to the pursuit of pleasure—Pythagoras adds that of contemplation. The philosopher, who is in charge of making such distinctions, assigns the highest life to that of thought pursued for its own sake. Philosophy is thus placed above politics. Philosophy, as contemplation, occurs with the *polis* but it is not of the *polis*. Honor and wealth are activities that take the *polis* as ultimate. Philosophy does not. The philosopher thus has a kind of freedom or independence, self-determination, the condition for which cannot be given by the state. Thus the situation becomes dangerous when philosophy attempts to affect the state. Unless the philosopher reduces philosophy to politics, which is the route frequently taken by modern schools of philosophy, the philosopher is placed in peril. When Plato says, in the *Republic* (which he reflects on, in the *Laws*, as describing a state only for the gods or children of gods), that a proper state requires that philosophers become kings or that kings take up the study of philosophy, he puts forth the irony upon which political theory rests. Although we can entertain such possibilities in a city in speech, neither will ever occur in political life. There is no room for contemplation in politics. Politics reduces everything to its own level, and when it cannot do so it becomes a dangerous beast, since politics is nothing but an exercise of power. The Leviathan acts bodily, not with the mind's eye.

Pythagoras's concept of philosophy is to speculate. The philosopher is the pure spectator. Diogenes Laertius, in relating the life and teachings of Pythagoras, writes that "Aristoxenus says that Pythagoras got most of his moral doctrines from the Delphic priestess Themistoclea" (8.8). For the Presocratics, the object of the love of wisdom is to secure a knowledge of nature, of the earth, heavens, and gods, not of human nature. The Platonic Socrates redefines philosophy. The *Phaedo*, the dialogue that presents the famous death scene and last conversation of Socrates, is related by Phaedo, one of the friends of Socrates present at the prison in Athens when he drank the hemlock. The details of Socrates' last day and death are told by Phaedo to a group of Pythagoreans who are residing in Phlius since their expulsion from southern Italy. Phaedo stops off at Phlius in the Peloponnese on his way home to Elis. He speaks with Echecrates, who asks him to relate these details because "hardly anyone from Phlius visits Athens nowadays, nor has any stranger come from Athens who could give us a clear account of what happened, except that he drank the poison and died, but nothing more" (57b).

Much of the dialogue is taken up by Phaedo telling of an elenchus between Socrates and the Pythagoreans Simmias and Cebes, who are from Thebes, another city in which the Pythagoreas settled following their departure from Italy and Croton. The subject is the possible lines of argument in which the immortality of the soul might be proved. It is ironic that on the day of his death we find Socrates searching for grounds to support the belief in the immortality of the soul, all of which are inconclusive. In the digression in the middle of the dialogue, Socrates declares the nature and purpose of the true philosopher, stating that "those who rightly philosophize are practicing to die [*hoi orthos philosophountes apothneskein meletosi*]" (67e). He underscores this later by characterizing philosophy, when pursued in the right way, as "practice of death [*melete thanatou*]" (81a).

The reason the dialogue takes place as a report made by Phaedo in Phlius, spoken to an audience of Pythagoreans, with Socrates conversing with two Pythagoreans, is that it concerns a redefinition of philosophy. The attention of philosophy is shifted from the essence of the physical world to the essence of the human. Philosophy, and only philosophy, can provide the wisdom necessary to confront the single problem of human existence—the mortality of the individual. Neither the gods nor the non-rational animals apprehend their own existence as problematic. Only rational animals do so.

The claim that the purpose of philosophy is to provide us with a way to confront our mortality is tied to the other Socratic pursuit, that of self-knowledge. If Pythagoras was thought to have obtained his moral precepts from the Delphic oracle (which may or may not be true), Socrates obtains his directly from the inscriptions on the *pronaos* of the Temple of Apollo at Delphi—*gnothi seauton* and *mēden agan*—know thyself and nothing overmuch. At the beginning of the *Phaedrus*, Socrates is asked by Phaedrus whether he believes the myth to be true that Boreas, the personification of the North Wind, abducted Orithuia, the daughter of the Athenian king Erechtheus, while she was playing with Pharmaceia in the Ilisus—at a spot quite close to where they are then conversing. Socrates says he has no time to seek the solution to such questions because anyone who applies his ingenuity to explain this legend "will have to go on and give a rational account of the form of the Hippocentaurs, and then of the Chimera; and a whole flood of Gorgons and Pegasuses and other monsters, in large numbers and absurd forms."

To make the mythical accounts involving these creatures rationally plausible, Socrates says, will require a great use of ingenuity and a great deal of time. Socrates says, "But I have no time for such things; and the reason my friend, is this. I am still unable, as the Delphic inscription orders, to know myself; and it really seems ridiculous to look into other things before I have understood that." Socrates says he will go along with what is generally believed in these matters because the truth or falsity of them is not the central issue for us as human beings. As mentioned earlier, he says, "I look not into them but into my own self. Am I a beast more complicated and savage than Typhon, or am I a tamer, simpler animal with a share in a divine and gentle nature?" (229c–230a).

Does Socrates' love of wisdom, which has turned his thinking from the rational examination of nature of his predecessors to the rational examination of human nature, show him to be a multiform beast like Typhon, a bundle of passions and appetites, or is he, through his use of reason, moving his psyche toward the divine? Is his reason a divine light within him, causing him to stand between the animal world and the world of the gods? This question is not psychological but metaphysical, requiring an answer that explains human nature in terms of its place within the whole of all existing things in the universe.

From Myth to Logic: Homer's Similes and Empedocles's Comparisons

In attempting to bring forth the idea of metaphysics, I have been following Vico's dictum that "doctrines must take their beginning from that of the matters of which they treat" (NS 314), which echoes Plato's claim in the *Timaeus* that "in every subject it is of utmost importance to begin at the natural beginning" (29b). This manner of contemplation is in accord with Aristotle's advice, quoted earlier, that to recollect requires that we obtain a beginning. To this principle of beginning at the beginning we may add a second observation by Vico, that those who wish to understand metaphysics should begin with the fact that metaphysics "seeks its proofs not in the external world but within the modifications of the mind of him who meditates it" (NS 374). For Vico, we engage in metaphysics not out of the strength of mind but out of its weakness, that is, when we apply the mind's eye to what there is, we do not perfectly apprehend it in its being as the really real, the *to ontos on*.

F. M. Cornford, the scholar of classical philosophy, traces, in *From Religion to Philosophy*, the starting point of Greek philosophy in the magical-mythical worldview that precedes the Presocratics. He holds that what "they called *physis*, and conceived as the ultimate living stuff out of which the world grew, could be traced back to an age of magic actually older than religion itself. In that first age, it was not as yet a representation at all, but a real fact of human experience, namely the collective consciousness of a group in its emotional and active phase, expressed in the practices of primary sympathetic magic."[4] The Presocratic philosophers or physicists come forth when mimetic rites cease to capture this original power of nature and infuse it into collective consciousness. This primordial power then begins to appear as an other, something that is not in ourselves as a cohesive force of human collectivity.

Cornford says, "Because it is not ourselves, it wears the negative aspect of a moral power imposing constraint from without; and this power, projected into the universe, leads to the conception of a supreme force, above Gods and men, in which Destiny and Right—*Moira* and *Dike*—are united."[5] A primordial group of humans to which this force appears can take this force into themselves such that it becomes the medium of their kinship. Out of the representations of this force arise the notions of group-soul and daemon, and from these develop the concepts of individual soul and personal deity. In this connection we might recall Socrates' daemon that he discusses in the *Apology*, and which appears to him elsewhere, in Plato's dialogues.

On Cornford's analogies, "The philosophers, one and all, speculated about the 'nature of things,' *physis*; and the *physis* about which they speculate

4. Cornford, *From Religion to Philosophy*, 124.
5. Ibid.

is nothing but this animate and divine substance."[6] The various schools of the Presocratics do not take thought outside of this original datum. They are physicists, not in the sense of making scientific observations and descriptions of natural phenomena, as we find later in the treatises of Aristotle, but in the sense that they refine and shift the properties and various senses of this medium of all things. Thus it becomes water in the thought of Thales, etc. Cornford's fundamental insight as to the proper reading of Presocratic doctrine is that of philosophy as a rational inquiry through a reformulation of myth. "The work of philosophy thus appears as the elucidation and clarifying of religious, or even pre-religious, material. It does not create its new conceptual tools; it rather discovers them by ever subtler analysis and closer definitions of the elements confused in its original datum."[7]

The method of myth is what Claude Lévi-Strauss calls *bricolage*. The maker of myth is a *bricoleur*. Like a handyman, the myth-maker responds to the world by forging what is needed or wished by reordering what is already there. The mythic mentality is fascinated with connecting and re-connecting the elements already present in the continuum of things. No sense of the new or the novel is relevant to the mythic mind. In contrast, on Lévi-Strauss's view, the scientific mentality is directed toward finding or projecting something new, something not previously known. The mythic mentality wishes only to re-know, in ever-varying patterns, the known.[8]

Philosophy originates as metaphysical speculation that begins as a transformation of mythical *bricolage*, guided not by imagination but by reason, in the sense that the Presocratics move beyond images to ideas. *Eidos* is used by the Presocratics in the sense originally found in Homer—as "what one sees," "appearance," or "shape" of a thing. In their use of it, *eidos* and its cognate, *idea*, come to be broadened into the abstraction of "characteristic property," linked to power or dynamics, meaning the "constitutive nature" of something. In so doing the mind gains distance from what is given it through the senses. At the level of mythic mentality, there is no fundamental awareness of the distinction between "seems" and "is." All is grasped and formed as interacting parts of a single field of immediacy. Knower and known are on the same plane of reality. The epistemological distinction between knower and known is parallel to the metaphysical distinction between seems and is.

6. Ibid., 125.
7. Ibid., 126.
8. Lévi-Strauss, *Savage Mind*, chap. 1.

In Anaxagoras, who is the eminent proponent of *nous* among the Presocratics, *nous* is a cosmological principle. It initiates motion and is like the soul; it is an intelligent and purposeful principle in the universe and is immanent within it, as the soul is within the body. *Physis* is replaced by *nous*. At the point of the Platonic philosophy, *noēsis* or "intellection" becomes the power of mind, corresponding to the *eidē* as the object of its knowing. *Noēsis* or the organ called *nous*, like *eidos*, has roots in Homer as a psychic awareness that passes beyond the power of sensation (*aisthesis*) and perceives the less tangible resemblances and differences between things.

Bruno Snell, in *The Discovery of the Mind*, illuminates the passage of thought from myth to logic. He calls attention to Empedocles as the figure who passes from the similes of Homer to the formulation of logical comparisons. The writings of Empedocles, Snell says, offer us the best evidence for the change from the poetic form of thought to the philosophic. Homer and Empedocles both employ similes, but to very different ends. As Snell puts this employment, regarding Homer, "The Homeric similes, i.e. those that concern themselves with actions rather than properties, are based on metaphors from verbs . . ." Examples are: "Athena *gilds* Odysseus with grace, Odysseus *drills* the trunk into the eye of the Cyclops, the girls *wheel* about in dance and so forth. The success of these similes is dependent on their ability to describe a slice of life in motion. This is true of the other similes, as when the attacking Hector is likened to a lion, the enduring hero stands like a rock in waves, etc."[9]

Homeric similes enhance a particular figure or action. They do not rise to a general sense of comparison. Although Empedocles writes in a manner employing similes, they transcend the particulars being compared. Snell offers an example of Empedocles's comparison of the properties of a lantern so constructed as to prevent the flame in it from being extinguished by the wind, but with walls of horn so thin as to allow the light to pass through. Empedocles then writes "just so at that time (when the eye was created) the primeval fire hid itself in the round pupil, enclosed in membranes and delicate covers, cut through with wondrously wrought straight passages, that kept back the depth of the water flowing round about; but the fire they allowed to pass through to the outside, because it was much more subtle."[10] The metaphors are not used to intensify a particular event and make it into a more elaborate image. The purpose of Empedocles's comparison is

9. Snell, *Discovery of the Mind*, 214–15.
10. Quoted in ibid., 214.

completely general, an explanation of a fact. The fact that light, but no air, can penetrate the walls of the lantern is due to the same physical properties that allow the eye, with its pores, to allow sight to pass to the outside but to contain the water in the eye. As Snell puts it, "Empedocles compares the one event with the other, and makes them one; the result is the same uncompromising insistence upon identity which underlies our saying that of two animals each is a lion."[11]

Cassirer makes a similar point in his discussion of language as a symbolic form, in referring to Lotze's theory of a "first universal" or "qualifying concept formation" (*die qualifiizierende Begriffsbildung*) (PSF 1:282–83). In this first universal, the particular is not subsumed under a class concept. Instead, the particular is raised to a universal by typing it in terms of the quality attached to it. Thus in a given primordial language there will be no word for a particular animal that expresses what it has in common with other instances of the animal. Each state of the animal will be given an individual name, signifying, perhaps, whether it is standing, sitting, lying, close by, far away, etc. In the development of language, Cassirer points out, often a prefix is added to the names of these states such that what is common to them begins to be articulated.

In Empedocles's example of the light of the lantern and the light of the eye, "he is not talking about a single man [carrying the lantern] or a particular object or a unique moment, but about a fact which is valid always and everywhere. The nucleus of Empedocles's similes is a *tertium comparationis*; they make sense only as precise statements of what both units of the comparison have always exactly in common."[12] Once the comparison is grasped as a *tertium comparationis*, the poetic character of Empedocles's metaphor and its setting is lost.

Empedocles's description of a man carrying a lantern is not about a particular man but something that is true of man as such and of the human eye as such. Empedocles has not caused us to feel or sense an object more concretely. He has explained it. We can now think it as a fact. We become its knower, placed at a psychic distance from it as an object that is known. Language at this point begins to manifest its logical and discursive character. The poetic becomes only a route to this standpoint, which allows reason to come forth as the medium of thought.

11. Ibid., 215.
12. Ibid.

The Heliconian Muses and Metaphysics

The intermediary between myth and metaphysics is poetry. The poet depends upon the mythic image for the formation of the poetic image. Homer retells the stories of the gods and in so doing takes his inspiration from the presence of the Muses, who are the Greek deities of poetry, literature, music, and dance—later to be associated with astronomy, philosophy, and all intellectual pursuits. Homer, the poet of poets, begins the *Iliad* with reference to these deities: "Rage—Goddess [*thea*], sing the rage of Peleus' son Achilles" (1.1). With the rage of Achilles and his conflict with Agamemnon told, the Muses appear by name at the end of Book 1, singing to the lyre of Apollo at the banquet of Hera, Zeus, and the other gods (1.601.4). The *Odyssey* begins with the line, "Sing to me, Muse, of the man of twists and turns driven time and again off course, once he had plundered the hallowed heights of Troy" (1.1–2). The nine Muses appear in the last book of the *Odyssey*, leading the dirge of the mourning and funeral in the telling of the death of Achilles (24.60–62).

Besides such passages in Homer, the first we hear of the Muses is their description in Hesiod's *Theogony*, which commences with the line, "Let us begin to sing from the Heliconian Muses, who possess the great and holy mountain of Helicon and dance on their soft feet around the violet-dark fountain and the altar of Cronus' mighty son [Zeus]" (1–4). As Hesiod tells us, the Muses were born of the union of Mnemosyne (Memory) and Zeus, who copulated for nine nights, and when a year had passed, Mnemosyne bore nine maidens who came forth with "a spirit that knows no sorrow."

In addition to their grace and spirit, the Muses possess this power: "they know how to sing many false songs similar to true ones, but they know, when they wish, how to proclaim true things" (25–28). Hesiod says they taught him the art of beautiful song, which includes this grasp of the interconnection of the true and the false. Another power the Muses have, and that they communicate to the poets, is "to tell of what is, what is to come, and what was before in a harmonizing voice" (36–38). The Muses not only interrelate the true and the false, they order time, because their mother is Memory. The presentation of time, the condition of our mortality, originally flows from the Muses. The ancient poet and seer are one, taught by the Muses how to comprehend time and thus how to apprehend the human condition.

Cornford describes in *Principium Sapientiae* how early Greek philosophy from Pythagoras through Plato brings together three types of figures—prophet, poet, and sage—and that this threefold configuration is not formulated as a novel theory but is a transformation of the primordial phenomenon of the shaman and shamanism. The philosopher becomes the successor of the seer-poet. Cornford says "that the wise man, whether called by his older title *sophistes* or by the more modest term 'lover of wisdom', was still recognized in the fifth and fourth centuries as one of the differentiated types which has emerged from the complex prophet-poet-sage. . . . His affinities have been ignored by modern historians of philosophy whose minds have been obsessed by the nineteenth-century 'conflict of religion and science.'"[13] The universal figure of the shaman and his practice of divination echoed in the power of the Muses to foretell in their songs underlie philosophy, and specifically metaphysics.

Vico, with his doctrine of "poetic wisdom," sees this point with clarity when he says, "Wisdom among the gentiles began with the Muse defined by Homer in a golden passage of the *Odyssey* [8.63] as 'knowledge of good and evil,' and later called divination. . . . The word 'wisdom' came to mean knowledge of natural divine things, that is, metaphysics, called for that reason divine science" (NS 365). Metaphysics that stands in the center of the practice of the love of wisdom is then a form of divination performed by the intellect.

In Plato's *Cratylus*, Socrates says, "As for the Muses and music and poetry in general, they seem to have derived their name from their eager desire [*mōsthai*] to investigate and do philosophy" (406a). In the *Theatetus*, Socrates says, "we have in our souls a block of wax" the condition of which may vary from one person to another. He says, "We may look upon it, then, as a gift of Memory, the mother of the Muses" (191c–d). The Muses keep us from forgetting because their arts preserve for us what they portray of the nature and harmony of the human soul. They impress what they portray on our memory. In fact, their name means as much, at least if we attend to Plutarch: "All the Muses are said to be called *Mneiai* [Memories]" (*Quaest. Conv.* 9.14).

In the *Phaedrus*, Socrates tells the story of the cicadas—that they were human beings before the birth of the Muses. When the Muses were born, song was first created. Some of the people were so overcome by the pleasure of singing they forgot to eat or drink. From them comes the race of the cicadas that, when born, burst into song and live without nourishment until at last they die. After death they go to the Muses to report who among

13. Cornford, *Principium Sapientiae*, 107.

the mortals has honored the Muses. "To Terpsichore they report those who have honored her by their devotion to the dance and thus make them dearer to her. To Erato, they report those who honored her by dedicating themselves to the affairs of love, and so too with the other Muses, according to the activity that honors each. And to Calliope, the oldest among them, and Urania, the next after her, who preside over the heavens and all discourse, human and divine, and sing with the sweetest voice, they report those who honor their special kind of music by leading the philosophical life" (259d). The Muses who first guide the poet pass on further to guide the philosopher.

In their primal art of song the Muses set the conditions of human life, in the sense that life is measured by past, present, and future. We can become the agent of their *mousikē*. Augustine says, "We do not measure poems by pages, for that would be to measure space not time; we measure by the way the voice moves in the poem" (*Conf.* 11.26). We know one thing of the nature of time, Augustine says: that it passes. We know that time passes because the mind has three kinds of acts. "The mind expects, attends and remembers: what it expects passes, by way of what it attends to, into what it remembers" (11.28). Augustine demonstrates this order of time by the example of reciting a psalm: "Suppose that I am about to recite a psalm that I know. Before I begin, my expectation is directed to the whole of it; but when I have begun, so much of it as I pluck off and drop away into the past becomes matter for my memory; and the whole energy of the action is divided between my memory, in regard to what I have said, and my expectation in regard to what I am still to say" (11.28).

Expectation and memory are the boundaries of the present, which is defined by my power of attention. Thus Augustine continues: "But there is a present act of attention, by which what was future passes on its way to becoming past. The further I go in my recitation, the more my expectation is diminished and my memory lengthened, until the whole of my expectation is used up when the action is completed and has passed wholly into my memory" (11.28). To give attention is to fix the moment when expectation passes into memory.

Augustine concludes, "And what is true of the whole psalm, is true for each part of the whole, and for each syllable: and likewise for any longer action, of which the canticle may be only a part: indeed it is the same for the whole life of man, of which all a man's actions are parts: and likewise for the whole history of the human race, of which all the lives of men are parts" (11.28). The psalm, the song in each of its parts and in its whole, is the structure of the whole life of a human being and of the whole history of the human race. What the Muses teach in the Greco-Roman world is taught in the psalm of the Judeo-Christian tradition.

Lévi-Strauss claims that myth and music "are instruments for the obliteration of time."[14] Implicit in this claim is that myth and music fit with the sense of the sublime as described by Longinus. Their effect, like that of genius in poetry or rhetoric, "is not to persuade the audience but rather to transport them out of themselves" (1.3–4). Myth and music transport the hearer out of time and into the sacred time, the time of the origin. Metaphysics as myth remembered is a denial of time in that its power to take the mind to the level of the universal suspends the temporal sequence of the finite. We master time in the song in that a song is always sung more than once. Its repetition is the means to suspend time. In like fashion, metaphysics is always a twice-told tale. We return over and over again to comprehend and contemplate a metaphysical truth. It is a truth only if we can repeat it and its repetition relieves us of the novelty of the particular. The universal requires memory for its continued existence in the mind.

As Francis Bacon says, in his account of vicissitude, "Solomon saith: *There is no new thing upon the earth.* So that as Plato had an imagination, *that all knowledge was but remembrance*; so Solomon giveth his sentence, *that all novelty is but oblivion.*"[15] Once myth is no longer a means to the formation of experience, we turn to metaphysics as the means to confront opposites and unite them in a narrative of thought. Metaphysics is a form of literature generated from the Muses' claim that they can sing true songs when they will. From the true and the false that are intermingled in the myth, metaphysics attempts to extract a dialectic of the true and the false such that the True is the whole—a complete speech of divine and human things and the causes of each—what Cicero defines as wisdom (*Tusc. Disp.* 4.26.57).

Our knowledge of Being begins, not in reason, but in mythical thought. Reason must begin from whence the first thoughts begin. No metaphysics can begin simply from reason, that is, without reason having an account of the origin of reason itself.

---

14. Lévi-Strauss, *Raw and the Cooked,* 341.

15. Bacon, "Of Vicissitude of Things," 451. See also Borges, "Immortal," 183.

Aristotle's *Protrepticus*

Finally, we may consider the question of whether it is possible to refrain from metaphysical thought—to declare simply that we may free ourselves from the burden of pursuing the questions of Being and learn to live without taking reason to such limits. Philosophical speech could perhaps be limited to the clarification of specific issues by the application of the techniques of logic to them. Further, such speech could be limited to formulating opinions concerning social and political issues regarding race, gender, and class. Philosophy could devote its time and energy to oscillating between technical issues and ideologies. In this way philosophy could claim a place in the world as just another form of thought. Indeed, much of contemporary philosophy occupies itself in these ways.

This manner of philosophizing allows us to formulate questions to which we can readily offer answers. Philosophy becomes fully professional, as described in Hegel's "*geistige Tierreich*," in which all are busy with the "*sache Selbst*" (PS 397; 285), the matter in hand. What is lost in this reduction of philosophical thought to opinion is the Socratic sense of the *logos*. In Socratic philosophical speech, the answer to any question is the pursuit of the answer. The philosopher who holds metaphysics as the heart of philosophy knows that the real always outstrips language. Plato makes this point in the famous passage in his *Seventh Letter*, by saying that he never wrote his philosophy down. "There is no writing of mine about these matters, nor will there ever be one. For this knowledge is not something that can be put into words like other sciences; but after long-continued intercourse between teacher and pupil, in joint pursuit of the subject, suddenly, like light flashing forth when a fire is kindled, it is born in the soul and straightway nourishes itself" (341c). The thought of the real itself remains esoteric beyond the power of speech, beyond logic, beyond opinion.

Once one's thought has crossed the threshold of philosophy and entered its realm there is no possibility of return. The necessity of philosophy is put in clear terms in Aristotle's *Protrepticus*. Along with Plato's *Seventh Letter*, it provides us with the most eloquent statement of the necessity of philosophy, understood as having metaphysics, that is, the problem of the real, at its center. Among the fragments from ancient authors relating to the early dialogues of Aristotle is this: "If you ought to philosophize you ought to philosophize; and if you ought not to philosophize you ought to philosophize; therefore in any case you ought to philosophize." A second sentence further elaborates this claim. "For if philosophy exists, we certainly

18

ought to philosophize, since it exists; and if it does not exist, in that case too we ought to inquire why philosophy does not exist—and by inquiring we philosophize; for inquiry is the cause of philosophy" (2:2416–17). This statement is one of the many renderings of the most famous passage in the *Protrepticus*, the original composition of which has been lost in its entirety.

The *Protrepticus* stands in a dialectical relation to the *Antidosis* of Isocrates and is imitated in the debate over the value of philosophy in Cicero's *Hortensius*. Isocrates' view of philosophy is opposite to Aristotle's view that contemplation is the goal of philosophic life. Isocrates insists that the pursuit of wisdom is the achievement of a life of temperance and just action. He says, "For since it is not in the nature of man to attain a science by the possession of which we can know positively what we should do or what we should say, in the next resort I hold that man to be wise who is able by his powers of conjecture to arrive generally at the best course, and I hold that man to be a philosopher who occupies himself with the studies from which he will most quickly gain that kind of insight" (*Antidosis* 271). Aristotle agrees with the importance of philosophy for the attainment of prudence, but he does not hold this pursuit to be the sum and substance of human wisdom.

Much of Aristotle's dialogue or "hortatory essay" (*logos protrepticos*) is in fact reconstructed from the *Protrepticus* of Iamblichus. On the passage regarding whether to philosophize, Quintilian says, "Sometimes two propositions are put forward in such a way that the choice of either leads to the same conclusion: for example 'We must philosophize (even though we must not philosophize)' ['philosophandum (est, etiam si non est philosophandum)']" (*Inst. Orat.* 5.10.70). If we apply Aristotle's conception of an *aporia* to Quintilian's formulation, then what philosophy produces is wonder (*thauma*). Philosophy is both a source of wonder about the nature of things and a source of wonder about its own nature.

Anton-Hermann Chroust, the composer of the reconstruction of Aristotle's *Protrepticus*, says its purpose is to be "an eloquent eulogy of speculative philosophy and an exhortation to live the 'philosophical life,' that is a life dedicated to speculative philosophy."[16] Chroust believes that the discussion of the interconnection of philosophic wisdom and happiness in Plato's *Euthydemus* is the likely source of Aristotle's main theme of the importance of the philosophic life in the *Protrepticus*. The discussion in the *Euthydemus* concludes with Socrates saying, "Since you believe both that it [wisdom,

16. Chroust, *Aristotle's Protrepticus*, xvii.

sophia] can be taught and that it is the only existing thing which makes a man happy and fortunate, surely you would agree that it is necessary to love wisdom [*philosophein*] and you mean to do this yourself." Clinias, the young boy whom Socrates is addressing, affirms, "This is just what I mean to do, Socrates, as well as ever I can." Socrates then declares, "When I heard this I was delighted and said, There, Dionysodorus and Euthydemus, is my example of what I want a hortatory argument [*protreptickon logon*] to be, though amateurish, perhaps, and expressed at length and with some difficulty" (282c–d).

In Chroust's reconstruction of Aristotle's text, the passage on the nature of philosophy reads, "The term 'to philosophize' (or, 'to pursue philosophy') implies two distinct things: first, whether or not we ought to seek [after philosophic truth] at all; and second, our dedication to philosophic speculation (*philosophon theoria*)."[17] Aristotle proceeds to elaborate on and extol the merits and nature of philosophy generally, saying, "The fact that all men feel at ease in philosophy, wishing to dedicate their whole lives to the pursuit of it by leaving behind all other concerns, is in itself weighty evidence that it is a painless pleasure to dedicate oneself wholeheartedly to philosophy."[18]

There is nothing in the history of philosophy to equal the *Protrepticus* as a praise of philosophy—except, perhaps, Cicero's praise, in his opening speech of the final part of the *Tusculan Disputations*: "O philosophy, thou guide of life, o thou explorer of virtue and expeller of vice! Without thee what could have become not only of me but of the life of man altogether? . . . To thee I fly for refuge, from thee I look for aid, to thee I entrust myself, as once in ample measure, so now wholly and entirely. Moreover one day well spent in accordance with thy lessons is to be preferred to an eternity of error" (5.2–5.6).

Cicero regards philosophy as the founding force of human culture and as supplying the wisdom necessary to live in a fully human manner. In this claim he places, as does Isocrates, prudence over contemplation as the center of philosophical endeavor. For Aristotle the philosophic life requires prudence, but prudence leads to and makes possible the ultimate goal of the philosophic life—contemplation. It is given that prudence is necessary for the conducting of human affairs, but is contemplation a necessity for human beings?

17. Ibid., 3.
18. Ibid., 24.

This is the question at the heart of the *Protrepticus*, and at the heart of philosophy and metaphysics, for philosophy, brought forward to the ultimate subject of comprehending being *qua* being, is the only field of thought that takes the meaning of its own existence as a central problem. When a physicist pauses to ask what physics is, the physicist is no longer engaged in pursuit of the knowledge of natural phenomena but is reflecting on the philosophical question of the place of physics in human knowledge. When the particular sciences in any of their forms turn to reflect upon what that science is, scientific investigation itself comes to a standstill. The production of any new philosophy is a redefinition of what philosophy is. It arises from grasping the nature of philosophy in a new way.

The claim of the *Protrepticus* places us in the position of a "Hobson's choice": an apparent freedom to take or reject something offered, when in fact no such freedom exists; an apparent freedom of choice where there is no real alternative. We find ourselves in the middle of this dilemma and we have no choice but to accept our position. We can at least affirm one thing: it is from this position that we must think of the nature of that which is the ultimate, the really real. Thus we learn from the start that there is no resolution to our position. It is a lifelong occupation.

2

The Ontological Argument
and the Complete Speech

The Argument

THE ONTOLOGICAL ARGUMENT FOR the existence of God was first formulated by St. Anselm, archbishop of Canterbury. In the first chapters of his *Proslogium*, he says, "For I do not seek to understand that I may believe, but I believe in order to understand. For this also I believe,—that unless I believe, I should not understand."[1] Anselm's argument in its essence consists of two premises and a conclusion:

> I can conceive in my understanding of a being greater than which none other exists.
> This being must exist in reality, independent of my conception of it, or it would not be the greatest such being.
> Therefore, God exists both in understanding and in reality.

Anselm exposits the meaning of the second premise by saying, "And whatever is understood, exists in the understanding. And assuredly that, than which nothing greater can be conceived, cannot exist in the understanding alone. For, suppose it exists in the understanding alone; then it can be conceived to exist in reality; which is greater."[2] Anselm, the believer, and the non-believer can agree that this definition of God is exactly what both mean by "God." God is the conception of a one and only being greater

1. Anselm, *Basic Writings*, 7.
2. Ibid., 8.

22

than which there is none conceivable. Thus the non-believer cannot argue that he is unable to have such a conception in his understanding because the non-believer must be able to conceive of God in order to deny God's existence. Is it possible, then, for the non-believer (the figure of the fool against whom Anselm places his argument) to assert the conception of a being greater than which none other exists and yet to deny its actual existence? As Anselm says, "For, it is one thing for an object to be in the understanding, and another to understand that the object exists."[3]

But in the case of one and only one being, Anselm holds, its conception necessarily entails its existence. He says, "For, it is possible to conceive of a being which cannot be conceived not to exist; and this is greater than one which can be conceived not to exist. Hence, if that, than which nothing greater can be conceived, can be conceived not to exist, it is not that, than which nothing greater can be conceived. But this is an irreconcilable contradiction."[4]

The contradiction occurs because we cannot both affirm the conception of a greatest being and at the same time deny an essential element of its greatness, namely, the affirmation of its existence. In advancing his argument, Anselm has completed the formulation of the Christian concept of God begun in Augustine's definition of God as a being "than whom there is nothing superior" (*De libero arbitrio*, 2.6.14). This definition could be held to refer to an entity that is not necessarily God. Anselm's argument adds to Augustine's definition that there is nothing conceivable that is greater than God. It is not simply that there is nothing superior to God; to conceive of something superior is not possible. Anselm's argument refines this metaphysical ultimate that thus guarantees the rational basis of monotheism. It removes any doubt that reason could bring forth.

It is not to my purpose to enter into the labyrinth of the criticisms and interpretations of the ontological argument. Instead, I wish to suggest a way in which its import may be grasped as the basis for metaphysics. We may say without complication that the ontological argument does not claim that because we can form a conception of something, what we have conceived exists. No one believes that this is the claim of the ontological argument. Its claim is that in one and only one case—the conception of the greatest thing—the conception implies its existence. The existence of anything less than the greatest thing is contingent, meaning that we can without

3. Ibid., 7.
4. Ibid., 8.

contradiction claim that the thing in question can also be conceived not to exist. In such a case existence is not a predicate. The subject involved in our conception either is or is not. The predicates we may attach to it, whether existing separate from our thought or confined wholly to it, simply express its attributes that constitute its particular nature.

"Existence" as it functions in Anselm's argument is of something existing non-contingently, that is, existing independently of the conceivable possibility of its not existing. The existence of a being greater than which none other exists is a being that exists necessarily. Charles Hartshorne, the most prominent modern supporter of the ontological argument, writes, "Anselm's intuition was that God exists in a superior manner, the ordinary way of existing being a defect, 'Thou dost exist so truly that Thou canst not be conceived not to exist,' and 'this is greater than a being which can be conceived not to exist.' Show me where the critics (Hume, Kant, e.g.) deal with this idea! They discuss whether or not what exists is greater than what fails to exist, which by any logic I know is not the same proposition at all."

I much agree with Hartshorne's analysis of the principle of necessary existence as distinguished from contingent existence. Hartshorne says further, "Since dollars or islands (the examples which have fascinated so many) are always conceivable as non-existent, there is no implication that existing dollars are greater than non-existent ones. The defect of contingency goes with being a dollar. . . . This king really is naked. The king is not Anselm's argument, or not that only; it is Kant's chief criticism of it."[5]

The so-called cosmological or "first cause" argument and the so-called teleological or "by design" argument are routes to take thought to the conception of the greatest being, but they both require the ontological argument to verify what is conceived to exist necessarily and independent of the conception. Does the ontological argument, then, succeed or fail? The argument fails in the sense that thought, through its rational means, is unable to prove the necessary existence of something standing outside the circle of thought defined by the two premises. Then why, we may ask, has the ontological argument held philosophical attention so strongly since its first statement by Anselm? We can agree with Hartshorne that there is no more famous philosophical argument than Anselm's so-called "ontological" proof for God's existence.

If we look at the argument not in purely logical terms, but add to these what we may call rhetorical terms, the genius of the argument can emerge.

5. Hartshorne, *Logic of Perfection*, 58–59.

It demonstrates a great truth about thought itself, namely, that to think of the greatest thing possible necessitates the second thought: that what is so thought must be thought to exist. It is the ultimate principle of the self-knowledge of thought. When thought is taken to its limit, it cannot but think of its object as actual. The ontological argument as Anselm formulates it does not leave the circle of thought. It demonstrates that the thought of God, of necessity, entails the *thought* of God's existence.

Of those figures in the history of philosophy who have given attention to the ontological argument, it is Hegel, and to an extent Spinoza, who saw its implications for the grounding of metaphysics in general, that is, who took the argument as more than an issue in philosophical theology. Hegel recognizes that there is no counterpart in ancient philosophy to the ontological proof. In his treatment of Anselm in his *Lectures on the Philosophy of Religion*, he says, "The proof passes over from the concept of God to the being of God. The ancients, i.e. Greek philosophy, did not have this transition; even within the Christian era it was not accomplished for a long time, because it involves the most profound descent of spirit into itself."[6] For the ancients—for example, Plato—the problem Anselm's proof purports to solve does not arise. Since *nous* is not itself a form but is compatible with the forms (*eidē*), both as it is in the world and as it is in human intelligence, there is no need to prove its reality. Its existence as the power of the mind's eye to see the forms and know them is given.

In Book Lambda of the *Metaphysics*, Aristotle says of thought, "The nature of divine thought [*nous*] involves certain problems; for while thought is held to be the most divine of phenomena, the question what it must be in order to have that character involves difficulties. For if it thinks nothing, what is there here of dignity? It is just like one who sleeps. And if it thinks, but this depends on something else, then (as that which is its substance is not the act of thinking, but a capacity) it cannot be the best substance; for it is through thinking that its value belongs to it." The activity of divine intelligence must be self-thinking. Perception, opinion, and understanding depend upon a separation of these capacities and on the object of which they think. But when thought takes place at the most excellent level, it has no object other than itself. As Aristotle concludes, "It must be itself that thought thinks (since it is the most excellent of things), and its thinking is a thinking on thinking" (1074b).

---

6. Hegel, *Philosophy of Religion*, 1:433.

The being of such thinking does not lie elsewhere. The being of this thinking is itself. Considered in this way, thought is a substance that conceives itself. As Hegel comments on Spinoza, "Spinoza says that substance includes being within itself. This inseparability of concept and being is only absolutely the case with God."[7] Faith claims that the representation of God is immediately conjoined with the being of God. The ontological proof claims to verify this union by reason.

As said above, the ontological argument fails if the being of the concept remains subjective, simply establishing the entailment of the being of the concept with the being of its object within the thought of its subject. The ontological proof, then, is an act of the thought of the understanding, not an act of the thought of reason. In the *Science of Logic*, Hegel says, "Now it might appear that the transition from the concept into objectivity is quite another thing than the transition from the concept of God to God's existence. But, on the one hand, it must be borne in mind that the determinate *content*, God, makes no difference in a logical progression, and that the ontological proof is only one application of this logical progression to that particular content" (SL 626; 354).

In other words, the concept (*Begriff*) itself has real being. The concept, whether of God or anything else, is alive, existing within the movement from subject to predicate in the speculative proposition (*spekulativer Satz*), as Hegel explains it in the preface to the *Phenomenology of Spirit*. There he takes "God is being" as his prime example of a speculative truth. "*Gott ist das Sein*" (PS 62; 51) affirms that (contrary to Kant's critique of the ontological proof) *Sein* is a predicate into which *Gott* as subject is dissolved. God "by itself is a meaningless sound, a mere name; it is only the predicate that says *what God is*, gives Him content and meaning" (PS 23; 22). Once God as subject becomes object through the predicate of being, the predicate must be taken back to grasp it as the content of the subject. God thus, in this dialectic, takes on life, the life of an internal movement.

What is true of God is true of anything thought because whatever is thought is in some sense also in existence. In this movement God ceases to be a fixed subject. Hegel says, "But of course the difficulty of finding *being* in the concept in general, and equally so in the concept of God, becomes insuperable if we expect being to be something that we find *in the context of external experience* or *in the form of sense-perception*, like *the one hundred dollars in the context of my finances*, as something graspable only by hand,

7. Ibid., 440.

not by spirit, essentially visible to the external and not the internal eye" (SL 627; 355).

In essence, Hegel claims that the ontological proof rightly grasped is nothing more or less than the possibility of metaphysical philosophy itself. The concept, properly comprehended as the medium of reason, always has being. This requires that substance must become subject (PS 17; 19). The dialectical inner form of the speculative proposition replaces that of reflective logic of the understanding, in which subjects are simply substances to which predicates are attached in order for them to fit into the classification of categories. Hegel says, "The customary practice of regarding the concept as something just as one-sided as abstract thought will already stand in the way of accepting what has just been suggested, namely, that we regard the transition of the *concept of God* to his *being* as an *application* of the logical course of objectification of the concept presented above" (SL 627; 355).

In the *Encyclopaedia Logic* Hegel adds, "For the concept, whatever other determination it may receive, is at least reference back on itself, which results by abolishing the intermediation, and thus is immediate. And what is that reference to self, but being? Certainly it would be strange if the concept, the very inmost of mind, if even the 'Ego,' or above all, the concrete totality we call God, were not rich enough to include so poor a category as being, the very poorest and most abstract of all."[8] The transition from thinking in terms of the understanding that is capable only of reflection to thinking in terms of reason that is capable of speculation, or the grasping of the inner form of the being of anything, is the master key to metaphysics.

Once Anselm's two premises are seen to rest on a dialectic upon which thought itself ultimately rests, God becomes the unavoidable first term of metaphysics. Anselm has found a way for us to obtain the very meaning of thought itself. When thought is applied simply to itself, the result is the absolute standpoint of thinking. We can then say there is no metaphysics without the ontological proof, whether it is affirmed explicitly or implicitly. The thought of the real entails the thought that the real is rational. Metaphysics presupposes the coincidence between thought and existence. When reason, through self-reflection, generates all the categorical distinctions of what is, the universals in the mind, thought is brought together with all of existence. The forms of thought are the forms of what is.

Once the centrality of the ontological proof is comprehended, in what way may it be meditated? If wisdom requires eloquence in order to speak,

8. Hegel, *Logic of Hegel: Encyclopaedia*, sec. 51 (108–9).

what form of eloquence is required of metaphysical thinking? Without eloquence, wisdom is mute or nearly mute, able only to offer logic without its counterpart of rhetoric. We can now turn to how the logic of the speculative sentence or proposition can be expressed in terms of intellectual narration. A great truth can never be simply affirmed. It must be embodied in the meanings that language can give it. As mythical thought originally narrates the real, metaphysical thought, now separated from this original speech, must narrate the real in its own words.

The Complete Speech

The ontological argument advanced in Hegelian terms allows for the formulation of the complete speech that is the aim of any true metaphysics. The original metaphysician is God, who makes by knowing and knows by making. Metaphysics is the divine science because it attempts to accomplish in language what God accomplishes in fact. The language of God is the distinctions that are within the real. The reality of the world is the actual complete speech of the Divine Maker. God does not speak about the things of the world; God literally speaks the things of the world. There is no separation between God's conception of anything and its reality. God begets what is.

What God makes, the metaphysician attempts to remake in rational narrative. But the first principle of this remaking is that the real always outstrips language. The complete metaphysical speech is noetic, but it can never capture its object as such. As the finger pointing at the moon, it is never the moon. Metaphysics as the ultimate activity of human reason originates from the weakness of mind, from mind's inability to make the truth of the real because it is unable to make the real itself. Any metaphysics, then, is only a likely story of the real, of being *qua* being. But the aim of any metaphysical narrative is to achieve an absolute speech of the absolute. The aim of any true metaphysics is not pluralistic, that is, simply to add another way of speaking about reality. True metaphysical speech is always tragic in the sense that it attempts to grasp the *aporia* between essence and existence and surmount it in its words, but the metaphysical speaker knows that this disparity can never be fully explained. The complete speech of the real, however, must still be sought because the self-knowledge of human existence requires its distinction from divine existence. Wisdom, that which the philosopher loves, requires the above-mentioned knowledge of things divine and human and the causes of each, as taught from the most ancient philosophers forward.

How, then, is the complete speech to be undertaken? Divine science cannot follow Descartes' doctrine of "the method for conducting right reasoning in the sciences." There is no specific problem to be solved that can be approached by finding a clear and distinct starting point from which to apply the distinction-making power of thought. Descartes' method is an embodiment of *ars critica* in that it sets a general standard by which a specific issue can be evaluated. Divine science requires what Vico calls a "new critical art." It requires that thought place *ars topica* prior to *ars critica*.

Ars topica is the finding of those ultimate distinctions upon which all else that can be understood reflectively depends. The art of finding these beginnings depends upon the power of metaphor. There is no known method for the production of real metaphors. The metaphor opens the world to us in a new way. Metaphor requires not method but that upon which method depends—*ingenium*—the power to see the similar in the dissimilar. It is the power of the Muses instilled in the mind's eye; it is the basic act of intelligence. The metaphysician shares with the poet the necessary flash of insight, the engagement of wit that yields the metaphor.

Any metaphysics, as Stephen Pepper has shown, depends upon a "root metaphor" that it expands into a system. By assuming a position independent from any one position, Pepper regards each type of metaphysics as a "world hypothesis." What a given metaphysics will allow as evidence for its account is subject to the terms that can be derived from the expansion of its root metaphor. "Root metaphor" is itself a metaphor, for it suggests that a metaphor can be a root from which a system of thought grows, as does a tree. A metaphysics is a tree of knowledge generated from its particular root that holds together the dissimilars of the world in its elaboration. But for the adherent of any root metaphor, the system that results is not a hypothesis. It is the True reached by the whole that is the system. Each of Pepper's root metaphors produces a complete speech.

Pepper identifies four metaphysical root metaphors. He says that his "aim is simple. It is to present the root metaphor and the set of categories of each of the four theories in its purest form, and to give some idea of the general appearance of the world as interpreted through each set of categories."[9] At the basis of all metaphysics is the philosophical imagination. As a poem unfolds around a master metaphor, often only implicitly

9. Pepper, *World Hypotheses*, 149.

present, so a metaphysics unfolds, not as an extension of the imagination to compound images, but as an extension of reason to compound ideas. But these ideas involve further images that are interwoven with them.

In regard to the interconnection of ideas and images we may add the observation of the French philosopher Michèle Le Dœuff, who in her analysis of the philosophical imagination says that although philosophy is characterized only in terms of the rational, the concept, the argued, the logical, and the abstract, it never is far from the image. She says, "Philosophical discourse is inscribed and declares its status as philosophy through a break with myth, fable, the poetic, the domain of the image. If, however, one goes looking for this philosophy in the texts which are meant to embody it, the least that can be said is that it is not to be found there in its pure state." In such texts, she says, "We shall *also* find statues that breathe the scent of roses, comedies, tragedies, architects, foundations, dwellings, doors and windows, sand, navigators, various musical instruments, islands, clocks, horses, donkeys and even a lion, representatives of every craft and trade, scenes of sea and storm, forests and trees: in short, a whole pictorial world sufficient to decorate even the driest 'History of Philosophy.'"[10] There is more to be said later about the general role of the image in philosophical speech. We have only to think of Plato's cave, Anselm's fool, Bacon's idols, Hegel's master-servant, or Wittgenstein's "family resemblance" to begin to comprehend Le Dœuff's point.

The first of Pepper's root metaphors is "formism" and specifically the sense of similarity that allows us to apprehend particulars in terms of the form they exemplify. "It is," Pepper says, "associated with Plato, Aristotle, the scholastics, neoscholastics, neorealists, modern Cambridge realists." The second type of metaphysic is "mechanism," the root metaphor of which is the "machine." "It is associated with Democritus, Lucretius, Galileo, Descartes, Hobbes, Locke, Berkeley, Hume, Reichenbach." It is connected to doctrines of "naturalism" and "materialism." These two types of root metaphor and the metaphysics that emerge from them are "analytical world theories." Being analytic means that they recognize facts or elements present in experience and the synthesis of these is something derivative. The two types that follow are "synthetic" in that they recognize complexes and contexts as primitive, and the analysis of these becomes something derivative. These two sets stand to each other as a polarity.

10. Le Dœuff, *Philosophical Imaginary*, 1.

The third type is "contextualism," which Pepper says "is commonly called 'pragmatism.'" He says "the best term out of common sense to suggest the point of origin of contextualism is probably the historic event." "It is," he says, "associated with Peirce, James, Bergson, Dewey, Mead. There may be a trace of it in the Greek Protagoras." It is likely Pepper has in mind the starting point of Protagoras's theory of knowledge, his famous contention that "man is the measure of all things, of things that are that they are and of things that are not that they are not" (*Diog. Laert.* 9.8). There is in this assertion a pragmatic element in that truth is related to human needs, to our ability to know how things are as they are and how they are not. Truth is a function of human activity.

The fourth type is "organicism." Pepper holds that there is no ordinary common-sense term that can be used to designate the root metaphor of organicism because "organism" is too loaded with biological connotations. He also rejects the term "integration" as a characteristic of the organic as, like organism, being too static. Metaphysics of this type focuses directly on the dynamic developmental and process-like character of the real. "It is," Pepper says, "associated with Schelling, Hegel, Green, Bradley, Bosanquet, Royce." Pepper says, "Actually, the historic event which is the root metaphor of contextualism is a nearer approximation to the refined root metaphor of organicism than any common-sense term."[11] The historical event cannot be comprehended in isolation, as a simple fact. It is part of a whole and a whole that is self-developing or self-determining. This whole is phenomenologically and logically prior to the individual historic event.

There are elements of all four of these types in any actual, complete metaphysical speech, but once described they provide a means to interpret such. If we look to the modern figures to be treated herein, the combination of the historic and the organic govern the speeches of Vico, Hegel, Cassirer, and Whitehead that are the subjects of the last four chapters of this book. Each of these figures faces the problem of how to make a complete speech about history and the real, how to bring together into language the whole of history with the whole of all that there is. It requires the coincidence of the contraries of human nature and nature. And to do so means to attain to some extent the perspective of the divine as that which governs both the cultural and the natural.

Metaphysical complete speech, because it is a speech of the whole of human experience, reflects in its language the three forms of symbolism

11. Pepper, *World Hypotheses*, 141–42, 232, 280.

that structure human consciousness—the image, the word, and number. These derive from the three functions of consciousness that Cassirer identifies in his phenomenology of *Erkenntnis* or knowledge—the expressive, the representational, and the "significative" (*Bedeutungsfunktion*). The image, the original form of which is mythical thought, is a picture, as Horace says of a poem. Images, as discussed above, are to be found throughout the great works of philosophy. The word is the element of ordinary language or common-sense thinking. The image is presentational, the natural achievement of the imagination. The image as the form of expressive consciousness is self-combined. Its meaning is within it. It is not an image *of* something.

The word is representational, the natural achievement of the formation of opinion. The meaning of the word of ordinary language is not present within itself, as is the meaning of an image; its meaning lies in its power to refer to the thing meant. What a word means is that to which it refers, whether it be a sensation, an internal feeling, a thought, or another word or phrase.

Number is the central example of "signification," in the sense of an element or variable in a system of elements or variables. Numbers, scientific formulas, and logical symbols are all such signifiers. In this regard, Whitehead says, "Philosophy is akin to poetry, and both of them seek to express that ultimate good sense which we term civilization. In each case there is reference to form beyond the direct meanings of words. Poetry allies itself to metre, philosophy to mathematic pattern."[12] Between poetry's meter and philosophy's mathematics lies common sense. In the complete speech all important points are ideally said three times—as an image, as what can be apprehended by common sense, and as a part of the distinctive categories or vocabulary of the particular metaphysical system itself. The threefold method of speaking, then, addresses all the basic functions of consciousness in the attempt to allow the mind access to the whole.

The happy or comedic aspect of the complete speech is this ability to speak in this comprehensive manner. The tragedic aspect of the complete speech is the fact that it can never conclude with the assertion "and that is all." The complete speech confronts all of the *aporiai* of experience but in principle it can never overcome the final *aporia* of the completion of its own intellectual narrative. At this point the metaphysical complete speech experiences its own version of the problem of consistency that Gödel's

12. Whitehead, *Modes of Thought*, 237–38.

proof raises for formal systems. Another way to say this is: it can never become the divine. Its speech remains human speech.

Kant is unable to live with this paradox—the fact that we can never have knowledge of the thing-in-itself—and so he retreats into a metaphysics of experience in order to gain a perfect circle of understanding. In so doing the Kantian philosophy misses the fact that the thing-in-itself is a concept that thought has of itself and its object. Subjective idealism breaks down in its lack of fortitude to keep speaking. Timidity of soul causes it to retreat into perfection and to settle for the complete speech of the understanding instead of the complete speech of reason. It is a failure of what Vico calls the "heroic mind," a failure to enter into the heroic act of mind that is willing to attempt the sublime speech of the paradox that lies at the base of human existence—that it is not fully but only partially divine.

Finally, we must consider that the speech of metaphysics, like that of forensic speech, must be persuasive. Quintilian says, "No one should think there is anything reprehensible in my suggestion that a Narrative which is wholly in our favour should be plausible, when it is in fact true. There are many true things that are not very credible, and false things are frequently plausible. We must therefore make just as much effort to make the judge believe the true things we say as to make him believe what we invent" (*Inst.* 4.2.34–39). The complete speech is guided by the Muses' musical principle to speak both truly and falsely but in so doing to also speak truly. The complete speech of a metaphysics is a series of partial truths and thus not the True itself, because what is partial is less than the whole truth. But the aim of the partial truths, their labor of the negative, is the True which is the whole. Philosophical speech is always forensic because it aims to convince the reader or hearer that its case is true and it can do so only if its case is in fact true.

Those who will look closely into the great canon of philosophies in the history of philosophy will see that their authors do not argue—except in a particular sense. Authors of total philosophies simply begin to speak and make distinctions. They resort to arguments along the path of their great narrative, but these are only to demonstrate the partial truths that lie within it. Overall, their complete speeches are likely stories, intended to take over the reader and lead the reader to the point at which the author is thinking. The proof of a metaphysics results only when the reader can make or re-make the system for himself or herself. Then the reader joins with the author or with several authors as having acquired a philosophical position from which to think. The reader attains then the divine pleasure the author provides—a specific route to contemplation and meditation of the True.

Logic of the Overlap of Classes

The logic of the complete speech embodies what R. G. Collingwood calls the "overlap of classes." As discussed above, Hegel has shown that in the ontological argument, in its movement from the first premise to the second, thought passes from the concept as subjectively apprehended to the concept as objective. Thus the ontological argument is internally dialectical. The subject and object poles are not two separate substances but opposites within the inner form of spirit or *Geist*. Thus the ontological argument is an ultimate principle of self-knowledge that governs a subject-object discursus. The complete speech is not a monologue of truth that separates itself from error. The partial truth of the subject is completed by the partial truth of the object. Both in their dialectical exchange constitute the True as the whole.

It is the ontological argument that distinguishes metaphysics from all the particular sciences. The object's existence for any particular science is separate from the conception of it and is that to which the thought of the science refers. The particular sciences divide the objects of experience into classes, which allow thought to produce judgments regarding their connections or disjunctions. When a judgment connects two classes as subject to predicate in ordinary logic, according to Collingwood, two assumptions are made. One is that the overlap of the classes will remain within a fixed limit; the second is that for any group of instances there is only one concept. Thus any two concepts that have a common extension are identical. Collingwood designates the first of these assumptions as committing "the fallacy of precarious margins." He designates the second of these as committing "the fallacy of identified coincidents."

Collingwood concludes that "these two fallacies are alternative applications of a single principle which, however true in exact and empirical science, is false in philosophy: the principle that when a generic concept is divided into its species there is a corresponding division of its instances into mutually exclusive classes."[13] He calls this "the fallacy of false disjunction," in that it involves the assumption that any instance of a generic concept must come under one or the other of its specific classes. The traditional

13. Collingwood, *Essay on Philosophical Method*, 49.

logical overlap of classes allows for only a partial overlap of classes; it does not allow for any instance to be fully a member of more than one class. But in order to make such a distinction we must presuppose that any instance is always more than itself. All things have multiple identities which are separated out abstractly in the doctrine of class membership of ordinary class logic. As Collingwood puts it, "The first rule of philosophical method, then, will be to beware of false disjunctions and to assume that the specific classes of a philosophical concept are always liable to overlap, so that two or more specifically differing concepts may be exemplified in the same instances."[14]

Only a dialectical logic governed by speculative reason is capable of structuring the philosophical sense of the overlap of classes. The static classification of the things of experience by means of reflective understanding presupposes Collingwood's sense of the overlap of classes. Dialectical logic shows that the identity of the members of any class is subject to self-development. It is a logic of metamorphosis. Ultimately, the guarantee of the philosophical sense of the concept is the fact that the two premises of the ontological argument are not the conjunction of two separate concepts. If it would be such a conjunction, then they would be also a disjunction and the concept of God would be separate from the concept of the existence of God.

The ontological argument, when rightly comprehended, shows that the two premises overlap—essence and existence, in the case of God, are necessarily the same. Since thought, in this one and only case, can demonstrate this overlap, it possesses the principle of reality itself. All that is less than God conjoins or overlaps essence and existence of its being in degrees of approximation to the absolute. The dialogic of true metaphysical thinking attempts to represent this overlap as it courses through experience of what is.

The doubling up of the overlap of classes is present in natural language in that words carry a double or multiple meaning. All words have etymologies. When one meaning of a word is intended, that is, when the word used is not intended as a pun, its other meanings are always implicitly present. They are there at a subconscious level, just below the overt meaning intended. In natural speech no word is ever capable of complete precision. It exists in a context and brings with it its own history.

To comprehend this characteristic of language, one need only turn to literature, to James Joyce's *Finnegans Wake*, in which every word both is and

14. Ibid., 49–50.

is not what it is. It is for this reason that this work defies common sense, which attempts to speak concretely by using the single meanings of words but instead speaks abstractly, overlooking the fact that every word is a valise that, when opened by its etymology, is an array of meanings. The metaphysician, like the poet, can use words in their multiple overlapping senses. But the interpreter most often is driven by the attempt to find consistency in the metaphysics under investigation. The interpreter too often hunts for the arguments and misses the speech that holds them in its process. The maker of the complete speech may have an element of the method Joyce claims to have used when he said, "Chance furnishes me what I need. I am like a man who stumbles along, my foot strikes something, I bend over, and it is exactly what I want."[15] The maker of a metaphysical complete speech is guided by consistency and coherence, but also by comprehension, and comprehension cannot be compromised by consistency and coherence.

The complete speech of first philosophy needs to be ideally both universal and genetic. It needs to claim that its principles and the assertions that derive from them are true without significant exception. And it needs to relate all that is in terms of origin and end. It should join *ratio* or the giving of an account with *narratio* or the giving of a narration. In so doing *oratio* is produced, the subject matter of which is the whole of all things. The *oratio* of first philosophy takes speech and thought beyond time. But it must fail, in that the attempt to transcend time is made within time and is thus subject to time. Any metaphysics attempting rightly to speak a truth beyond time finds itself to be another metaphysics, to be entered into the record of the history of philosophy.

But it cannot be a doctrine of historicism that governs the production of metaphysics. It is not good that metaphysics, in its denial of time, must fall prey to it. But it does, because as a divine science it is a science of the divine and not the divine itself. A way to put this, in terms of the ontological argument as the foundation of metaphysics, is that as in the argument, as said above, thought never leaves the circle of its own existence. Yet it is the most that thought can do, that is, thought can, through the argument, leave the bonds of its subjective existence for its objective existence. But its existence remains as thought and never as divine existence as such. There remains an *aporia* that cannot be overcome. The outcome of this tragedy is the peace of contemplation, of which Aristotle speaks. All that can be thought has been thought. No more remains that can be done.

15. Mercanton, "Hours of James Joyce," 213.

3

The Coincidence of Contraries

Learned Ignorance

ERNST CASSIRER BEGINS HIS monumental, four-volume study *Das Erkenntnisproblem in der Philosophie und Wissenschaft der neueren Zeit* (The problem of knowledge in philosophy and science in the modern age) with the claim that Nicholas of Cusa (1401–64) is the "founder and pioneer of modern philosophy."[1] The questions regarding the relation of God to the world that dominate the whole of the Middle Ages are reposed, in a new and objective form, by Cusanus. His views appear in their most concise and compelling form in *De docta ignorantia* (*Of Learned Ignorance*). At the center of this work is Cusanus's principle of *coincidentia oppositorum* that is connected to his concept of God as absolute maximum. This conception of God can be seen as a recasting of the ontological argument in that it is a conception we cannot avoid having. And once we acknowledge this fact of thought we are committed to the conception of the existence of its object. The existence of an absolute maximum is put forth by Cusanus, not as an article of faith, but as a necessity of thought, in order that thought can make distinctions regarding what exists—namely, the world.

Cassirer, in his *Individual and the Cosmos in Renaissance Philosophy*, states that "Cusanus had distinguished a threefold direction of the Absolute-Infinite, the pure Maximum which as such remains unattainable to the human intellect. And opposed to Him are two forms of the relative-infinite.

---

1. Cassirer, *Erkenntnisproblem*, 17.

One is present in the world, the other in the human mind."[2] The relative-infinite, as present in the world, is reflected in the conception of the universe as without spatial limits. The relative-infinite, as present in the human mind, is the recognition that the mind has no limits to the progress of its thoughts. The human mind, both in its thoughts about the universe and in its thoughts about itself, realizes that it cannot attain the form of the absolute maximum or absolute infinite. Thus it learns that it is in fact and in principle ignorant of the absolute's actual nature.

Cusanus begins modern philosophy by incorporating this principle of ignorance in the wisdom the philosopher seeks. It offers philosophy a new beginning. He expects his reader to see the parallel with Socratic ignorance—that with which ancient philosophy begins, or begins again. When Socrates calls philosophy down from the heavens, he transfers philosophy from its focus on nature, at the hands of the Presocratics, to a new focus, on human nature. To do so he introduces a new conception of wisdom—that the love of wisdom must begin with the realization that one does not know. One does not know even what kind of being the knower has, or that the solution to this quandary is to turn thought back upon itself, by asking others what they know. Socrates thus introduces the question as the medium of the love of wisdom. In this way, the *elenchos* is born as the method of philosophy, or "Socratic method."

Coupled with this method is the trope necessary to philosophical discourse—the trope of irony. Irony is the ability to speak about one thing while intending to lead thought to reach another thing. In the *Euthyphro*, Socrates questions Euthyphro, who is a religious expert, about the nature of piety or holiness—our proper relation to the gods. But in doing so Socrates is only secondarily interested in the definition of piety. His true purpose is to discover what it is to be human. Once the method of the question (which, to formulate, requires the acknowledgment of ignorance) enters philosophy, it is impossible for philosophy to return to being a pure spectator of nature. The love of wisdom becomes the love of self-knowledge.

The first chapter of Cusanus's famous work concerns "How it is that knowing is non-knowing." He says, "Both the precise combinations in corporeal things and the congruent relating of known to unknown surpass human reason—to such an extent that Socrates seemed to himself to know nothing except that he did not know."[3] Socrates, in his speech in the *Apolo-*

2. Cassirer, *Individual and the Cosmos*, 69.
3. Nicholas of Cusa, *On Learned Ignorance*, 50.

gy, raises the question of whether he possesses a certain kind of wisdom, as some have said. He asks, "What kind of wisdom? Human wisdom, perhaps. It may be that I really possess this, while those whom I mentioned just now [his accusers] are wise with a wisdom more than human" (20e). Socrates possesses human wisdom, in the sense that there is nothing in principle to prevent him from the pursuit of self-knowledge. But to possess divine wisdom would require that one is in fact divine, not human. Otherwise we are left with pretension and self-deception—thinking that one knows something that in principle one cannot know.

The question Cusanus wishes to answer is how we can comprehend why, in principle, we cannot have divine knowledge or complete knowledge of what is divine. We desire to know what we do not know. If we can fully attain a grasp of our own ignorance, that is, to know in some sense what we do not know, we will attain "learned ignorance." As Cusanus says, "For a man—even one very well versed in learning—will attain unto nothing more perfect than to be found to be most learned in the ignorance which is distinctively his. The more he knows that he is unknowing, the more learned he will be."[4] Cusanus's doctrine of learned ignorance tells us we must give up the method of reasoning to which medieval philosophy had become attached. Vico characterized this reasoning as a kind of "blind speaking . . . a cloying manner of reasoning, always in the same syllogistic form and quite spiritless gait, enumerating each order of discourse—*praemitto primo, praemitto secundo, obiicies primo, obiicies secundo*."[5]

In contrast to this Scholastic sense of proof and knowing, Cusanus places the concept that all knowledge is a process of proportion, of the adjustment of opposites. As Cassirer puts it, "The *De docta ignorantia* began with the proposition that all knowledge is definable as measurement. Accordingly, it established as the medium of knowledge the concept of *proportion*, which contains within it, as a condition, the possibility of measurement."[6] In Cassirer's view this sense of measurement puts Cusanus's thought in touch with Leonardo da Vinci's attitude toward method and the Renaissance approach to the world and nature in general. Cusanus, like Socrates, requires a new sense of method; it is not that of the *elenchos* or dialogue (which Bruno will exploit) but the use of the mathematical image to reach the idea of the absolute. Cusanus's approach to the absolute is an

4. Ibid., 51.
5. Vico, "Philosophy and Eloquence," 87.
6. Cassirer, *Individual and the Cosmos*, 51.

act of philosophical irony, in that what we learn, in taking thought to the limit of the absolute in order to overcome the relative infinity of opposition, is the impossibility of thinking the absolute as such, but, on the other hand, realizing that thought cannot dispense with what it cannot think.

The principle that ignorance is the basis of the pursuit of wisdom is central to the beginning of Renaissance thought. Petrarca's seminal essay *On His Own Ignorance and That of Many Others* is further testament to this claim. Petrarca quotes the line from one of Augustine's letters that is the source of Cusanus's title: "Brought before Thee and put next to Thee who art the Rock, their judges are overthrown and their learned ignorance has become manifest."[7] It is notable that Cusanus owned a copy of this writing of Petrarca.[8] Petrarca says that the ignorant cannot be the judge of ignorance. Instead, "It is the wise man who is entitled to judge ignorance as well as of wisdom and of anything whatsoever—wise, of course, he must be in the specific matter of which he is judging."[9] On this view, then, Socrates is correct in claiming he may be wise in human things. The master key to self-knowledge is to know that one does not know. Ignorance in this sense is distinctive to human beings, and not applicable either to animals or to the gods.

Absolute Maximum

The *Absolute* as a philosophical term first occurs in Cusanus's *De docta ignorantia* (1440) and was used by German philosophers regularly, after Kant, to refer to the idea of an unconditioned reality.[10] Cusanus used *absolutum* exactly in this sense as the term for God, conceived as a being that is not limited in its reality by anything else and is in no sense comparable to anything else. God's being is unconditioned in a complete and perfect sense.

There is nothing opposite to the Absolute or *maximum absolutum*. It is infinite, but not in the sense that its opposite is finitude. Finitude, the condition of human being as well as the being of all else in the world, is characterized by opposites. The oppositions within finite being always correspond to each other, but they are never brought together such that they

7. Petrarca, *On His Own Ignorance*, 64. The line is from Augustine's *Epistle* 130.15.28.
8. Petrarca, *On His Own Ignorance*, 64 n. 39.
9. Ibid., 66.
10. Inwood, *Hegel Dictionary*, 27.

can truly coincide, in the sense of forming a synthesis or unity. *Coincidentia oppositorum* is possible only in divine being, which is beyond all oppositions. The being of God is an undifferentiated actuality. The question Cusanus faces is whether it is possible in some sense to think such an infinite as an actuality that does not have the world in its infinitude as its opposite. As a thought, such an actuality is not an act of faith.

Cusanus says that our acknowledgment of learned ignorance concerning this ultimate sense of the being of the divine will lead us to find a way to think correctly about it. This thought will require a form of symbolism, as we cannot think the being of God directly, as an object. He then cites Anselm, claiming that "operating in this way, then, and beginning under the guidance of the maximum Truth, I affirm what the holy men and the most exalted intellects who applied themselves to figures have stated in various ways. The most devoted Anselm compared the maximum Truth to infinite rectitude. (Let me, following him, have recourse to the figure of rectitude, which I picture as a straight line.)"[11]

Cusanus is clear that his mathematical formulations are only means of symbolizing the absolute maximum. There is no mathematics of the divine as such, at least none that we could know. He says, "I maintain, therefore, that if there were an infinite line, it would be a straight line, a triangle, a circle, and a sphere. And likewise if there were an infinite sphere, it would be a circle, a triangle, and a line. And the same thing must be said about an infinite triangle and an infinite circle."[12] Thus beginning with the concept of an infinite straight line (a line that can be infinitely extended), a curved line that approaches it, if infinitely extended in its curve, would approach a straight line but never completely coincide with it. A *coincidentia oppositorum* of the two lines would never be possible. But the curved line would be infinitely approaching it. If this process is true of a curved line it is true of a circle, since it is no more than a closed curved line, and of a sphere, since it is no more than a three-dimensional circle. A triangle will infinitely approach the figure of a straight line if its sides are extended infinitely outward or inward in their angles. Cusanus also understands a sphere to be the result of a triangle and a circle, such that the two sides of the triangle are infinite lines, making an infinite circumference of an infinite circle.[13]

---

11. Nicholas of Cusa, *On Learned Ignorance*, 63.
12. Ibid.
13. Ibid., 66.

Cusanus turns to the sense in which a finite line is divisible and an infinite line is not. An infinite line is not divisible because it has no limits within which a division can be made, and a finite line is not infinitely divisible because it would then cease to have magnitude and would lose its essence as a line. Cusanus says, "By comparison, there is only one infinite line, which is the essence of all finite lines; and because of the fact that a finite line necessarily falls short of an infinite line, it cannot be the essence of itself, even as it cannot be both finite and infinite."[14] Cusanus's purpose is to demonstrate that the opposites of *maximum absolutum* and *contractum* can be seen to come together in God. If these opposites of all opposites can be so shown, then any opposites of any specific kind can be conceived as coinciding in the divine actuality.

There is no risk of pantheism, because God and the world cannot be understood as identical. The coincidence of the finite and the infinite is not possible in the world, in finite or divisible being generally. God's actuality is fully transcendent of the opposition of the infinite and the finite. Since we cannot comprehend the sense of infinity that is not an opposite to the finite, we can only remain in learned ignorance. We can grasp only symbolically, to some extent, the infinity of God's being. Cusanus's conception of God's being precludes the doctrine of analogical predication. We cannot predicate in any sense properties of the divine being. The reality of God's divine being does not differ by degree from created reality. We cannot apply any sense of measurement to the infinite nature of God.

There is no hierarchy of creation through which God's being can be assessed. Each thing in the world is equally at an infinite distance, in its being, from God's being, just as the curved line, when infinitely extended, remains an infinite distance from the straight line to which it tends. The fact that it is a curve is not overcome, no matter how great its extension. Cusanus has filled in Anselm's conception of the greatest being and shown, through his mathematical images, what such a conception entails. In so doing, Cusanus's ontology has established that finitude is defined by the existence of opposites and by the fact that they can never coincide, making finite being a dynamic actuality, one that is constantly in motion with itself. Yet this finite motion is not chaotic, because it is governed by the stability of the divine coincidence of all opposites.

Cassirer says, "This view exerted a *cosmological* influence only very much later, in the natural philosophy of the sixteenth century, and most

14. Ibid., 69.

especially in the philosophy of Giordano Bruno."[15] Cusanus's ontology establishes the idea of a self-ordering infinite that can be applied to understand both nature and the mind's activity.

Infinite Universe and Worlds

Bruno's cosmology presupposes the ontology of the infinite formulated by Cusanus. Bruno is influenced by the cosmological implications that Cusanus draws out, in the second part of his *On Learned Ignorance*, regarding the "conditions of the earth." Cusanus says that the earth is indeed in motion, even though we do not perceive it so. To realize it moves, we require a comparison with something fixed, as we do to perceive any motion of any kind. From any point where we were to place ourselves in order to measure the earth's motion in relation to the heavenly bodies, we would always think ourselves to be at the immovable center. Since all motion is relative, there is no true center. Cusanus concludes, "Hence, the world-machine will have its center everywhere and its circumference nowhere, so to speak; for God, who is everywhere and nowhere, is its circumference and center."[16]

Cusanus claims that the earth is not spherical as such but it tends toward sphericity. When an infinite line is contracted it can attain the perfect figure of a circle. He claims that the nearly perfect motion is circular and the nearly perfect shape is spherical. He concludes, "Therefore, the shape of the earth is noble and spherical, and the motion of the earth is circular; but there could be a more perfect [shape or motion]. And because in the world there is no maximum or minimum with regard to perfections, motions, and shapes (as is evident from what was just said), it is not true that the earth is the lowliest and the lowest."[17] Since the world does not have an absolute maximum or minimum, it also does not have a fixed middle point or an exact number of parts or divisions.

Bruno cites Cusanus's views, in this part of *On Learned Ignorance*, in regard to the question of multiple heavenly bodies. Bruno claims that there must be innumerable fixed suns or fiery bodies around which "there may revolve earths both larger and smaller than our own."[18] These multiple worlds are not identical to each other; they are comprised of diverse parts.

15. Cassirer, *Individual and the Cosmos*, 69.

16. Nicholas of Cusa, *On Learned Ignorance*, 117.

17. Ibid.

18. Bruno, *Infinite Universe*, 306.

Bruno agrees with Cusanus that the darkness of the earth, in comparison with the brightness of the sun, does not mean that the earth is more ignoble or in any way inferior. Each of the multiple bodies is composed of its own arrangement of elements and has its own character. Bruno says, "This honest Cusan hath known and understood much; he is indeed one of the most remarkably talented men who hath lived in our world."[19] Bruno does not endorse all the points of Cusanus's cosmology, but he has no disagreement with its central principles and claims, as he elaborates and modifies them.

In *Cause, Principle and Unity*, Bruno employs mathematical diagrams similar to those found in *On Learned Ignorance*. For Bruno as for Cusanus, these diagrams symbolize the coincidence of the absolute maximum and minimum such that the opposites of a curve and a straight line "coincide in the principle and the minimum, since (as the Cusan, the inventor of geometry's most beautiful secrets, divinely pointed out) what difference could you find between the minimum arc and the minimum chord? Furthermore, in the maximum what difference could you find between the infinite circle and the straight line?"[20]

All of Bruno's metaphysics is an elaboration of his cosmology. His cosmology begins from Copernicus, but Bruno goes beyond Copernicus. Copernicus in essence suggested a rearrangement of the solar system, but Bruno draws out the implications that the universe is infinite and that there are infinite possible orders of heavenly bodies. In *The Ash Wednesday Supper*, Bruno claims this may be so even if we are unable to see the movement of such distant bodies: "considering greater distances, and the largest and most luminous bodies (of which it is possible that innumerable others are as large and as luminous as the sun, and even more so). Their circles and motions, though very great, are not visible."[21] Bruno suggests that there are no fixed stars and spheres. The universe is an infinite system of internal relations of contraries.

In *The Expulsion of the Triumphant Beast*, Bruno says, "What I wish to infer is that the beginning, the middle, and the end, the birth, the growth, and the perfection of all that we see, come from contraries, through contraries, into contraries, to contraries. And where there is contrariety, there is action and reaction, there is motion, there is diversity, there is number,

---

19. Ibid., 307.
20. Bruno, *Cause, Principle and Unity*, 96–97.
21. Bruno, *Ash Wednesday Supper*, 205–6.

there is order, there are degrees, there is succession, there is vicissitude."[22] In *On the Infinite Universe and Worlds*, Philotheo, who speaks for Bruno, says, "You see further that our philosophy is by no means opposed to reason. It reduceth everything to a single origin and relateth everything to a single end, and maketh contraries to coincide, so that there is one primal foundation both of origin and of end." The origin in its potency is all that there is or ever can be. The origin is also the end; they form a circle. Philotheo concludes, "From this coincidence of contraries we deduce that ultimately it is divinely right to say and to hold that contraries are within contraries, wherefore it is not difficult to compass the knowledge that each thing is within every other."[23]

The movement of the universe as a whole is a macrocosm that acts as a receptacle of multiple microcosms of the same movement of contraries that are imitations of the two ultimate contraries that comprise the whole that, in the terms of Cusanus, are the *maximum absolutum* and *contractum*. Because the whole of the universe is a coincidence of the contraries of its beginning and end, it is an ultimate approximation to divine reality. In *Cause, Principle and Unity*, Bruno says, "Hence, every potency, every act which, in the principle, is (so to speak) enfolded, united and unique, is unfolded, dispersed and multiplied in other things."[24] Thus each entity is a constant circle of potency and act in which the act always becomes a new potency, continually passing beyond itself. What it is, is at the same moment what it is not, that is, what it may come to be. What a thing is not has content because what it is not, it can be, in the development of its motion.

Bruno says, "The universe, which is the great simulacrum, the great image and sole-begotten nature, is also all that it can be, through the very species and principal members, and by containing the totality of matter, to which nothing is added, nothing taken away, of complete and unified form." The universe is, then, the one true individual, the only thing that is wholly complete in itself. But being complete, it is not perfect, because what it is, is constantly in the process of becoming what it is. Its internal motion never completes itself; it never comes to its own perfection. Its being is becoming. Bruno concludes, "But it is also not all that it can be, because of its very differences, its particulars, its modes and its individuals. It is only a shadow of the first act and the first potency, and, in consequence, potency

22. Bruno, *Triumphant Beast*, 90–91.
23. Bruno, *Infinite Universe*, 369.
24. Bruno, *Cause, Principle and Unity*, 66.

and act are not absolutely one and the same thing in it, since one of its parts is all that it can be."[25]

The first act and first potency is the act of divine making. In this act these contraries complete each other perfectly. Nature, however, is a shadow of the absolute synthesis of potency and act. Nature is continually in a state of this transformation of contraries, and this process of becoming can never cease. Thus nature is not identical with the divine, which is reality itself. Nature is thus like the divine but not identical with the divine. Bruno's position is not a pantheism, as it has been falsely described. Nature has the divine as its contrary, but the divine does not have nature as its contrary; the divine is the perfect principle of potency and act, the perfect circularity on which nature depends for its self-identity and existence. The self-contained infinite of the divine, for Bruno as for Cusanus, is a coincidence of opposites that cannot be realized in nature.

Bruno's cosmology maintains that the celestial bodies of the universe have their own principle of animation. This principle is intrinsic to their being. In *The Ash Wednesday Supper*, Bruno says, "For, if we reflect, we will find that the earth and many other bodies, which are called stars and are the principal members of the universe, inasmuch as they give life and nourishment to the things which derive their substance from them and likewise give it back to them, they [the stars] must all the more so have life in themselves. By means of this life, they move according to an intrinsic principle toward the things and through the spaces appropriate to them, with an ordered and natural will."[26] In *On the Infinite Universe and Worlds*, Bruno refers back to this point in *The Ash Wednesday Supper*, saying that all of the celestial bodies "move by the internal principle of their own soul . . . wherefore it is vain to persist in seeking an extrinsic cause of their motion . . . we prove that this earth doth move from innate animal instinct, circle around her own centre in diverse fashion and around the sun."[27]

Celestial bodies, then, are alive because they have their own principle of intrinsic motion. They are animals. They are not inert substances or simply physical matter. Bruno's metaphysics is a theism that distinguishes the infinity of God from the infinity of worlds, which are finite centers of animation. Bruno makes this clear, saying, "So that the Prime Origin is not that which moveth; but itself still and immobile, it giveth the power to

25. Ibid.
26. Bruno, *Ash Wednesday Supper*, 155.
27. Bruno, *Infinite Universe*, 266–67.

generate their own motion to an infinity of worlds, great and small animals placed in the vast space of the universe, each with a pattern of mobility, of motion and of other accidents, conditioned by its own nature."[28] Bruno's metaphysics of divine infinity and infinite worlds is on the threshold of a functional rather than a substantive account of the relation of finite to infinite. The finite and infinite are not two separate substances that interact. They are aspects of the same self-determining actuality. The coincidence of these contraries, while imperfect in the motions of nature, make the universe what it is. Bruno's cosmology, developed solely through his own reasoning, is remarkable for its modern sense of nature as a self-process of interrelations of events.

Dialogic Thinking and the Love of Wisdom

As mentioned earlier, there are two ways to think a thing and say it: in the manner of *ratio* and in that of *narratio*. In the complete speech, as also described earlier, these tend to combine in *oratio*. *Ratio* is the rhetoric of the Scholastics. Behind the interlocking arguments of the disputation and the formulas of the *summa* is the list, the drawing up of an account that eliminates all chance of inconsistency or paradox.

Bruno presents his philosophy in dialogue. The dialogue is a particular form of the narrative in that, like a narrative, it has beginning, middle, and end. But into the narrative it introduces the idea of the theater, the *theatrum mundi*, the sense of the world as a stage in which thought takes place. In facing the reader with a dialogue, Bruno is causing the reader to recall the Ancients against the Scholastics. The dialogue is the invention of the Platonic Socrates, but Aristotle begins his career, as with the *Protrepticus*, by writing dialogues, as discussed earlier. Among the Romans, Cicero has figures speaking their thoughts to each other.

In the dialogue we are asked simply to look upon thought, to engage in *theōria*, *theōrein*, the term from which *theater* is derived and which, in Plato and Aristotle, comes to mean "contemplation." We are asked to enter into contemplation, looking on with our mind's eye, and to comprehend the whole of what is said in its various aspects without concern for any subsequent act of doing or making.

The dialogue is ancient and it is Renaissance. In the dialogue nothing is simply proved; instead, views are questioned and other views are

28. Ibid., 267.

projected. Thus the dialogue is the natural form of speculation. The reader is asked to consider things in a certain way, to see if one set of thoughts is not more plausible than another. In the dialogue the reader is asked to make the truths recalled therein for himself, along with the participants. In the dialogue the love of wisdom is pursued as a process among thinkers. The thinker is a social animal, at least among other thinkers.

Descartes, with his forms of discourse and meditation, sets the style of modern philosophy as the soliloquy, the philosopher speaking alone in the study, pronouncing the results of thought for others to consider. It is a short step to the practice of the modern presentation of the philosophical paper. The results of investigation of some topic are announced and offered for inspection. Questions concerning its correctness are forthcoming, but, unlike the Socratic question, they lead nowhere. They just put forth problems. Criticism replaces speculation. The modern age, as Kant said in his preface to the first edition of the first *Critique*, is especially an age of criticism, and "to criticism everything must submit."[29] Under such conditions speculation becomes not simply unfashionable but impossible. The engagement in the dialogue encourages the likely story, the speculative oration of Socratic thinking. In speculation, thought is trying to see itself—the philosophic pursuit of self-knowledge. In speculation, thought is never far from the leading or root metaphor and the questions that can be generated from it.

The four examples of metaphysics in the modern world, in the chapters that follow, are not expressed as dialogues. Yet they are not extended examples of Cartesian soliloquy. Their spirit is Socratic, in that they are speculative. They purport to say the most that can be said about the human, the natural, and the divine. In so doing the reader is drawn in, in dialogic fashion, to attempt to make the truth that is made for him or herself. In this sense the orations that are these systems are implicitly dialogic; at least, they allow the reader to approach them in this way. They do not leave the reader's thinking the same, once the reader has entered them. They contain clues for the readers as to how to make the system for themselves.

Philosophy can renew itself only when it returns to its attachment to wisdom, which requires the reaffirmation of the principle of ignorance. This grand act is not to be found in the modern forms of philosophy known as postmodernism, deconstructionism, liberation philosophy, or in race, gender, and class theory. These mistake critical thinking for philosophy. They are hollow at their core because they divorce *ars critica* from *ars*

29. Kant, *Critique of Pure Reason*, 9n.

topica. Ars critica is nothing by itself. It requires first the pursuit of the True that lies only in the beginning, the origin—that which *ars topica* seeks. This sense of wisdom can be pursued only by knowing that one does not know. These modern forms of philosophy only know that they know. They ask no questions. They only criticize the narratives they claim that others hold, believing that Socrates' art was that of criticism. They are humorless and sincere, bereft of irony. All bad philosophy, like all bad poetry, is sincere. Nothing can come of their efforts because, while hollow at the core, they insist on their great vitality and originality, full of sound and fury.

The opposite of "sincere" in philosophy and the arts is not "insincere." It is irony. Irony offers self-determined distance from the matter at hand. Sincere poetry or philosophy always implicitly knows that its images or ideas are sentimental and precious. This knowledge is the "bad faith" of sincerity. To protect them, the author of the work will attempt to force them upon the audience, often with aggressive attitudes and unvarying claims. Often these claims are in fact nothing more than political or ideological commitments. Sincerity, in its desire toward self-protection, insists on reducing all thought to its own level. The openness that irony brings to thought is a threat.

In this forceful sincerity there is no acknowledgment of the touch of folly that Erasmus finds and portrays in all human endeavor. It is the ironic possibility of folly that keeps a work human and allows us to contemplate it rather than simply be pressed to support it. In fact, if we enlist in its sincerity our support is never enough because its sincerity is not provisional. Only complete acceptance will do. The greatest foe of bad or sincere philosophy is the Socratic question. The Socratic question asks the obvious. It asks the position to account for itself, to open itself to the ironies of inquiry. Sincerity will then be unable to carry the day by the constant insistence on the great meaning of the views placed in question. The Socratic question frees us from taking ourselves too seriously.

The four metaphysical philosophies that follow presuppose the ancient and Renaissance principle of ignorance as the basis of wisdom, and place *ars topica* before *ars critica*. They offer us a metaphysics of history, the idea, the symbol, and process. Each of these combines *ratio* with *narratio*. And each realizes and causes us to realize that the purpose of intellectual narrative is to combine and recombine opposites. The True lives through the self-movement of opposites, as does life itself. In each of these four, we confront the pursuit of self-knowledge. They are all neo-Socratic philosophies.

Each of these four metaphysical systems is a whole university. One can find in them, in principle and to a large extent in detail, a grasp of all that there is. Each of these systems, when penetrated by the reader, is a complete metaphysical education, a complete education in the topic of the really real. Metaphysics, as it is often approached, far too quickly dissolves into arguments in which thought can easily confine itself. To speculate is to see more broadly than any argument can provide. Metaphysics is first of all a kind of seeing of the world that can, in specific ways, incorporate arguments. Simply to amass arguments about the actual will never provide the whole which is the True. Thus I recommend that the mind's eye be allowed to wander in these systems and to see their sights. In this way we may follow Socrates' advice and not be an enemy of argument, but realize there is more to philosophical speech and metaphysical vision than can be held within the bonds of argument. Metaphysics is a high form of literature, an exercise of letters that can take us from the image to contemplation.

4

The Providential Order of History

The True Is the Made

GIAMBATTISTA VICO (1668–1744) IS generally regarded as the founder of the philosophy of history. Among the ancients there are great writers of history, and philosophers who hold historical views, but we do not encounter there a fully developed philosophy of the history of all nations. Vico's formulation of the common nature of the nations is the subject of his best-known work, the *Scienza nuova*, published in its definitive edition in 1730 and revised in the year of his death. My aim in this chapter is not to present an essay bringing together the various elements and sources of Vico's thought.[1] It is instead an attempt to identify those parts of Vico's views that contribute to the topic of metaphysics.

Vico saw his new science of history as a metaphysics. In his introduction to the *New Science* Vico says, "This New Science or metaphysic [*questa Nuova Scienza, o sia la metafisica*], studying the common nature of nations in the light of divine providence, discovers the origins of divine and human things [*cose*] among the gentile nations" (NS 31). Vico's *New Science*, then, is a doctrine of wisdom, in accord with Cicero's and Varro's views before him. Vico, like Socrates, professes a knowledge of human things but not a knowledge of the divine as such. Like Socrates, Vico knows the difference between the human and the divine. He has a knowledge of the divine as present in human affairs, but he professes no divine knowledge. In defending his metaphysics against critics, he states, "I come to a halt in

1. For a comprehensive account, see Verene, *Vico's New Science*.

the contemplation of the supreme Creator. I show Him to be the 'Deity' because with a nod or, better, with instant effects, He wills and with His creative act He speaks. So that the works of God are His words."[2] God knows by making and makes by knowing, an act, the nature of which, is closed to the human. Regarding the deity as such, Vico engages in learned ignorance.

Karl-Otto Apel, in his study of language in humanism from Dante to Vico, calls Vico "a conclusion, indeed the Owl of Minerva of Italian Renaissance culture."[3] Ernesto Grassi, in his study of the rhetorical basis of philosophy in the humanist tradition, holds that in Vico "the whole humanist tradition reached its highest philosophical consciousness."[4] Although not a Renaissance figure, Vico preserves the wisdom of humanism in the age of post-Cartesian metaphysics.

Having completed his education, much of which was based on self-directed study while a tutor to children of the Rocca family at their castle at Vatolla, south of Naples, but also having received a doctorate in both civil and canon law, Vico found himself facing a wall of Cartesian thought. As he says in his autobiography, "With this learning and erudition Vico returned to Naples a stranger in his own land, and found the physics of Descartes at the height of renown among the established men of letters. That of Aristotle, on its own account but much more because of the excessive alterations made in it by the schoolmen, had now become a laughingstock."[5] He says that metaphysics, which in the sixteenth century had commanded the attention of minds in the highest rank of literature, was now thought to be suited only to study in the cloisters. The great revival in Italy of poetry, history, and eloquence prominent in ancient Greece, along with the philosophy of Plato, the medicine of Galen, and the study of the Greek language, commanded no interest. In other words, what Descartes in his *Discourse* had precluded from his method of right reasoning had in fact been put aside in the discussions in the academies and salons of Neapolitan intellectual life.

In his first published book, *On the Study Methods of Our Time*, Vico argued for a theory of education that would strike a balance between the humanistic achievements of the ancients and the natural scientific achievements of the moderns. He was, in fact, still insisting on the importance of this point in the last academic address of his career: "I hold the opinion that

2. Vico, "First Response," 127.

3. Apel, *Idee der Sprache*, 320–21. My translation.

4. Grassi, *Rhetoric as Philosophy*, 37.

5. Vico, *Autobiography*, 132.

if eloquence does not regain the luster of the Latins and Greeks in our time, when our sciences have made progress equal to and perhaps even greater than theirs, it will be because the sciences are taught completely stripped of every badge of eloquence."[6] He adds that for all that Cartesian philosophy claims to have corrected, by its geometric method, from Scholastic forms of reasoning, it has no ability to allow its adherents to comprehend the whole, for such comprehension requires eloquence (the ability to speak of probabilities and to course through the whole of a subject), which the step-by-step method of geometric reasoning precludes.

It is not enough to confront Descartes' philosophy with a theory of education based on the general distinction between the ancients and the moderns. In 1710, Vico projected a philosophical system in three parts: a metaphysics, a physics, and an ethics or moral philosophy. Vico completed only the first of the three, with the unexpected title, *On the Most Ancient Wisdom of the Italians Drawn Out from the Origins of the Latin Language.*[7] The second part may have corresponded to an essay Vico wrote one year later on the equilibrium of animate bodies, which is now lost. The third was never written.

The strangeness of Vico's title can be overcome quickly, once it is evident that Vico is posing another sense of "firstness" or origin against Descartes' generation of first principles through hypothetical doubt. Descartes' sense of "firstness" is geometric: that metaphysical thought should begin from axioms that are demonstrated to be self-evident. This is an atemporal, deductive, or logical sense of firstness. Vico's sense of firstness is genetic or historical. What is first is *principium* or beginning. Since we are not at the beginning of the first metaphysical thoughts of humanity, we must draw them out or unearth them from the oldest meanings in the most antiquated language to which we have direct access.

Vico says that the Latin language abounds in learned expressions that could not be reasonably ascribed to the earliest Romans, the formulators of Latin, because those peoples were wholly concerned with military affairs and with agriculture. They were soldiers and farmers. These learned expressions that Vico will draw out in his analysis must have entered early Latin from other nations. Vico says, "As for learned nations from whom they could have received these expressions, I can find two: the Ionian and

6. Vico, "Philosophy and Eloquence," 87.

7. Vico, "Proem," in *Ancient Wisdom*, 5–7.

the Etruscan."[8] The metaphysical distinctions Vico finds in ancient Latin are imported from the Ionian philosophers and physicists and the natural theology in it derives from the Etruscans, who were experts in sacred rites and religious observances. Vico says, "I conjecture with certainty that the learned origins of Latin words came from these two peoples, and for this reason, I have focused on drawing out the most ancient wisdom of the Italians from the origins of the Latin language."[9]

Etymology takes us to the beginnings of words and the beginnings of words take us to the beginning of mind. Metaphysics must start where thought itself begins. It is not incidental that Vico admired the *Cratylus* most among Plato's dialogues. To recover this original wisdom will provide us with a real beginning point that is concrete. It will stand against the abstract and artificial method of Descartes. Descartes' procedure of hypothetical doubt provides us with only the stamp of certainty that we in fact know what we know—that I exist, God exists, and the world exists. But we have no knowledge of how we know this. We have no knowledge *per causus*. Vico will show how we know what we think we know, by demonstrating how we have come to know it. He will show us the original insights by which thought has come to establish what is. It is a scandal to logic that logic cannot provide us with the truth of its starting points. Descartes attempts to overcome this scandal by applying the law of non-contradiction to thought itself—but the result is a vacuous certainty.

The fundamental claim and theme of the *Most Ancient Wisdom* is this: "For the Latins, *verum* (the true) and *factum* (the made) are interchangeable or, as is commonly said in the Schools, they are convertible."[10] Thus: *verum est ipsum factum* and *verum et factum convertuntur*. To this principle we may add Vico's distinction between *scientia* and *conscientia*. Geometric and mathematical reasoning generally are *scientia* because such truths are made from their principles. Mathematical truths are true because we make them. The object of mathematical knowledge is itself. Reasoning about the natural world is *conscientia* because the objects of our knowledge are not made by the knowing mind itself. This is why, Vico observes, experiment is the key to the natural sciences. In experiments we come as close as possible to making what is known. *Conscientia* (conscience or consciousness) may best be understood as "witnessing consciousness." Natural science,

8. Ibid., 5.
9. Ibid., 7.
10. Ibid., 17.

54

through its procedures, is an elaborate and precise witnessing of what God has made.

God makes by begetting. The objects of nature of which natural science seeks to make a knowledge are begotten by God. The divine mind has no distinction between knowing and making. To know divinely is to be able to produce the object known and to be able to do so is what it means to be God. God is both omniscient and omnipotent. But God is not identical with the world. The divine mind's relation to itself is beyond the comprehension of the human mind.

Having delineated these three senses of knowing and making in the *Most Ancient Wisdom*, Vico applied his *verum-factum* principle to the making of historical knowledge or knowledge of the world of nations in the *New Science*. He says, "Now, as geometry, when it constructs the world of quantity out of its elements, or contemplates that world, is making [*si faccia*] it for itself, just so does our Science [make for itself the world of nations], but with a reality greater by just so much as the things having to do with human affairs are more real than points, lines, surfaces, and figures are" (NS 349).

Vico claims that the new science is constructed by a geometric method and he does initially present it as involving 114 axioms. His method is "geometric" in the sense that from this collection of axioms he derives a great number of conclusions concerning the common nature of the nations. But his science is more specifically geometric in the sense that his metaphysics stands to the human world in the same way mathematics stands to the natural world. History is applied metaphysics as natural science is applied mathematics.

Human beings are capable of making a knowledge of the historical world of nations because they have originally made this world themselves. We make up the originating principles of mathematics and from these we make mathematical truths. In so doing the human mind confronts itself. Because our actions have made history, we are able to make a knowledge of history, a *scientia*. In doing mathematics and metaphysics in this sense, we are imitating the activity of the divine mind. Vico's *verum-factum* principle is an epistemological embodiment of the Renaissance doctrine of microcosm and macrocosm.

God makes the world and in it man makes history as a manifestation of human nature. Human nature itself is not made by humans, it is begotten by God. Thus as human beings make their world they are subject to divine providence. Just as there is a divine order to the world of nature, there is a providential order to the world of nations. For human beings to make a knowledge of history they must recognize the divine or providential order in history. The self-knowledge that human beings acquire by formulating the common nature of the nations includes a knowledge of the divine. But it is only a knowledge of the divine as object. Human beings do not become God in history. They can only transform into a process of rational thought what is begun in the mythic mind as divination—the taking of auguries and reading the signs of the heavens. Through making a science of history, human beings can arrive at a knowledge of providence, the actions of God in the human world. The new science is a *scientia* in relation to history but it is a *conscientia* in relation to God.

Metaphysical Method

Metaphysics is by its nature a science of first principles. It is Vico's purpose, in the *Most Ancient Wisdom* and in the *New Science*, to show that Cartesian philosophy is not a science of first principles. To accomplish this demonstration Vico needs simply to show that Descartes' *cogito* is not a true first principle, and as such only an abstract and defective metaphysics can follow from it.

In the *Meditations on First Philosophy*, Descartes, having considered the grounds for doubting his existence—the possible deception of his external senses, his internal sense of his own condition, and the logical possibility of an evil genius or divine deceiver that could cloud even his intellect—asserts the certainty: "*Ego sum, ego existo.*"[11] Then he asks, "*Sed quid igitur sum? Res cogitans. Quid est hoc?*"[12] Putting these together is Descartes' so-called *Cogito ergo sum*, "I think, therefore I am" argument. Seen as an argument, it is a second-order enthymeme, the minor premise suppressed.

Fundamentally, it is a metaphysical transformation of the logical law of non-contradiction. The law of non-contradiction cannot be proved because it is the very condition of any proof. It has its unique status as a principle of thought because it must be affirmed in any attempt by thought to deny it. Any attempt by thought to deny the existence of "I think" requires the affirmation of the existence of it. As Descartes says, it is necessarily

11. Descartes, *Meditationes*, 7:25.
12. Ibid., 28.

true whenever I conceive it. But the self-proof contained in the *cogito* argument stops at this point. To proceed with his metaphysics, to assert the existence of God and the world, Descartes must define what thinking is. He answers his own question of what a thinking thing is by treating it as a genus comprising various species of thought. He says a thinking thing (*res*) is a thing that doubts, understands, affirms, denies, wills and is unwilling, imagines, and has sensory perceptions. None of these claims about the nature of thinking is proved. They are simply claimed to be a definition of thinking—and thus properties of a thinking being.

The common precedent for Descartes' *cogito* principle is Augustine's "*si fallor, sum*" (*De libero arbitrio* 2.3.7). Apparently, in arriving at the argument of his first principle, Descartes did not think of this formulation in Augustine; at least, this is what he claims in a letter from Leiden in November 1640. Descartes writes, "I am obliged to you for calling to my attention the passage of St. Augustine to which my I think, therefore I am [*Je pense, donc je suis*] has a rapport. I have been to the library of this town today and find that truly he does use it to prove the certitude of our existence."[13] Descartes says he is happy to be in such company and that this first principle could have fallen from the pen of anyone.

Vico, although unaware of this letter, shows that Descartes' view, that this principle could have fallen from the pen of anyone, is certainly the case. He turns to the *Amphitryon* of the Roman comic dramatist Plautus. At the beginning of the play (441–47), while Amphitryon, the commander of the Theban army, is away at war, he is cuckolded by Jupiter, who has assumed his guise. The guise is so perfect that Amphitryon's wife, Alcmena, innocently presumes the disguised Jupiter to be her husband. In this comedy of errors and false identities, Mercury, accompanying Jupiter, assumes the guise of Sosia, the slave of Amphitryon. Now returned with his master from war, Sosia finds his perfect double, and begins to doubt his own existence when Mercury insists that Sosia is mistaken about his own identity. He says to Sosia, "Oh, you can have the name when I don't want it; *I'm* Sosia and you're nameless." Sosia then looks into a mirror, and seeing himself, says, "But, when I think, indeed I am certain of this, that I am and have always been [*Sed quom cogito, equidem certo sum ac semper fui*]."[14]

---

13. Letter CCXIX, November 1640, in Descartes, *Oeuvres de Descartes*, 3:247.

14. Vico likely quotes this line from memory. Plautus writes, "*Sed quom cogito, e quidem certo idem sum qui semper fui*" (447).

In the Cartesian critical literature, I have found no discussion of this passage in Plautus as being a precedent. Plautus puts in the mouth of a slave, as a comedic line, what Descartes presents as the highest of metaphysical principles. In fact, Vico concludes that Descartes' certitude of the *cogito* is "commonplace knowledge available even to a person without any learning, like Sosia, not some rare and exquisite truth which requires the meditation of a great philosopher to invent."[15]

Vico's fundamental criticism is that Descartes' *cogito* principle does not answer skepticism because no skeptic doubts his own thinking. Instead the skeptic professes his skepticism with complete certainty. Descartes' certitude and that of the skeptic are one. Their certitude is mere consciousness (*conscientia*), not science (*scientia*). Vico says, "So even though the skeptic is conscious that he is thinking, he does not know the causes of thinking, or on what basis thinking comes to be."[16] Vico says the "I" that is thinking is both a body and a mind; thus if I, as a thinking being, were the cause of myself, my thinking or mind would be the cause of my body. As human, both body and mind are the cause of my thinking. Otherwise, I would be nothing but mind, which would make me not human but divine. Vico says, "What is more, thinking is not the cause of the fact that I am a mind, but only a sign of it, and a *techmerion* (indication) is not a cause; and no prudent skeptic ever denied the certainty of indications, only the certainty of causes."[17]

A metaphysics that cannot overcome skepticism is finally flawed, and in Descartes' case his metaphysics is flawed from its very beginning. His hypothetical doubt and his answer to it is no answer to real doubt because certainty is not knowledge. We must seek a new beginning point for metaphysical thought that relies on more than logical maneuvering. Any metaphysics that cannot confront skepticism tends toward either dogmatism, in the sense of simply claiming what it holds is true, or pluralism, in the sense of only claiming to add yet another perspective to perennial problems. One of the most prominent axioms of Vico's *New Science* is that "doctrines must take their beginning from that of the matters of which they treat" (NS 314). It is, perhaps more than any other axiom, what governs Vico's new science.

As cited earlier in the preface, Vico, in an addition to the *New Science* written after its publication in 1730, entitled "Reprehension of the

15. Vico, *Ancient Wisdom*, 33.
16. Ibid.
17. Ibid.

Metaphysics of René Descartes, Benedict Spinoza, and John Locke," says, "For the metaphysics of the philosophers must agree with the metaphysic of the poets [the original makers of mythical thought], on this most important point, that from the idea of a divinity have come all the sciences that have enriched the world with all the arts of humanity: just as this vulgar [poetic] metaphysic taught men lost in the bestial state to form the first human thought from that of Jove, so the learned must not admit any truth in metaphysics that does not begin from true *Being* [*l'Ente*], which is God."[18]

The nature of Vico's claim will become more evident in the discussion of his conception of "poetic metaphysics" that follows. This topic is preceded, in the *New Science*, by a section on "Method," in which Vico replaces the Cartesian conception of method as critical thinking with that of topical thinking. It is not enough to criticize Cartesian metaphysics; a metaphysical method must be brought forth that replaces the Cartesian.

Vico's method is derived from the Muses, the goddesses who govern the arts of humanity, the very arts that Descartes dismisses. Vico says, "Indeed, we make bold to affirm that he who meditates this Science narrates to himself this ideal eternal history so far as he himself makes it for himself by that proof 'it had, has, and will have to be' [*dovette, deve, dovrà*]" (NS 349). To meditate (*meditare*), for Vico, is to narrate (*narrare*). Narration is to comprehend something in terms of its beginning, middle, and end, to understand it as alive, animate, yet with equilibrium. The equilibrium is the presence of providence in the course of what is to be understood. Thus Vico modifies the power of the Muses, to tell of what was, is, and is to come, as a purely temporal order into a necessary order of causes such that it had, has, and will have to be.

Vico's science, like the activity of the Muses themselves, is based on memory. It is a science of recollection. Vico defines memory, as does Aristotle, as the same as imagination ("*la memoria è la stessa che la fantasia*" [NS 819]). Memory as the science of the Muse takes three different aspects, namely, "memory [*memoria*] as it remembers things; imagination [*fantasia*] as it alters or simulates them; ingenuity [*ingegno*] as it encompasses them and puts them in order and arrangement" (NS 819; my translation). All memory originates in the senses. What is sensed and remembered is formed by the inward power of the imagination and what is so formed is integrated with the other contents of memory.

18. Vico, "Reprehension," 179–80.

Vico arrives at the principle of ideal eternal history (*storia ideal eterna*) and at the narration of this history itself by means of memory. He transforms the unique conception in Roman law of *ius gentium* (the law of peoples or "nations") from a static principle that regards whatever part of the laws of all peoples that is also common to Roman law as an actual, natural law into a dynamic principle of the pattern of development common to all the nations. Thus Vico holds that all nations exemplify a course and recourse of three ages—the age of gods, of heroes, and of humans. What each nation or gentes has in common with every other nation is this pattern, although each nation develops at a different temporal rate. This order of three ages is the presence of providence in history.

Vico says, "The decisive proof in our Science is therefore this: that, since these [human] affairs have been established by divine providence the course of the affairs of the nations had to be, must now be, and will have to be such as our Science demonstrates, even if infinite worlds were born from time to time through eternity, which is certainly not the case" (NS 348). Vico's reference is to Bruno's cosmology of infinite worlds, which he denies is the case. But why should he bring up this point? Bruno is heretical, and, as the Inquisition was actively, but unofficially, functioning in Naples, Vico is quick to deny this possibility. By raising this point Vico is asserting that, as history is the elaboration of human nature, which is divine and governed by providence wherever we might conceive humans to be, they would be subject to ideal eternal history and hence to his science.

Another aspect of Vico's method is its combination of philosophy and philology. Philosophy, most notably metaphysics, pursued apart from its presence in the new science, presents us with the true (*il vero*). The purpose of philosophy is to know what is universal and thus it errs by half in not producing the thought of the whole. Philology, for Vico, is the knowledge of all things that depend on human choice, "all histories of the languages, customs, and deeds of peoples in war and peace" (NS 7). Philology offers us a knowledge of the certain (*il certo*). The philologians or historians have failed by half by not guiding their investigations by universal principles. To produce the new science, "philosophy undertakes to examine philology" (NS 7). Bringing these two forms of thought together, Vico says, gives us a "new critical art" (*nuova arte critica*), in which philosophy and philology act as correctives to each other. Vico also calls this philosophical-philological method a "metaphysical art of criticism" (NS 348).

Narration is governed by the art of the Muses, that is, governed by the principle of *verum-factum*, in the sense that history is first made (*factum*) and then the knowledge of it is made (*verum*) by its narration in accordance with the *ius gentium* of ideal eternal history. In the *Universal Law*, Vico asserts a second major principle, that "the certain is part of the true [*Certum est pars veri*]."[19] This is the principle that underlies his philosophical-philological method. Any civil law is something made by human choice or authority. Such a law is a certain, not in the Cartesian sense of something indubitable but in the sense of something particular that is made. For such a law to be truly law (*lex*) it must be part of Law (*ius*) or its authority is simply ideological, subject to whatever power exists to enforce it. Law in its universal sense as a human institution must be what is right and reasonable. The authority of Law is reason itself that, on Vico's view, is in accord with the divine as invested in human nature. All of Vico's *New Science* is an enactment of *ius gentium*, in which the particulars of the life of the nations are brought together under the universals of human nature.

In his autobiography Vico says Plato shows us man as he should be and Tacitus shows us man as he is. Vico says "that the wise man should be formed both of esoteric wisdom such as Plato's and of common wisdom such as that of Tacitus."[20] Vico brings these two together under the Christian idea of providence. To do this, Vico requires a doctrine of the origin of humanity, a doctrine of the first thought as it first appears. He finds this in what he calls "poetic wisdom" (*sapienza poetica*). He says, "We find that the principle of these origins both of languages and letters lies in the fact that the first gentile peoples, by a demonstrated necessity of nature, were poets who spoke in poetic characters. This discovery, which is the master key of this Science, has cost us the persistent research of almost all our literary life" (NS 34). The master key to this science, then, is the discovery of the truly first thought, and with this discovery we will attain what is needed in a first philosophy or metaphysics, a comprehension of being *qua* being as an original human act.

Poetic Metaphysics

Cassirer says, "Giambattista Vico may be called the real discoverer of the myth. He immersed himself in its motley world of forms and learned by

19. Vico, *Universal Law*, 1:100.

20. Vico, *Autobiography*, 139.

his study that this world has its own peculiar structure and time order and language. He made the first attempts to decipher this language, gaining a method by which to interpret the 'sacred pictures,' the hieroglyphics, of myth."[21] The seventeenth-century natural-law theorists—Grotius, Pufendorf, Selden, and Hobbes—did not recognize that the myths of the ancients and also those of contemporary primitives and peasants were vestiges of a mentality and manner of life that existed at the origin of human society and from which modern society developed in stages. They saw the origin of society as a simple opposite to the modern state, a state of nature that, in Hobbes's characterization, was a war of all against all that was overcome by the enactment of a covenant or social contract.

It was Vico's insight that humanity as a whole developed, like each human individual, through a series of ages. The adult first comes into being as a child. It was also Vico's insight that forms of thinking and ways of acting are interlocked in this development. Plato, in Book 3 of the *Laws*, has a picture of the origin and development of society, but it is not filled out in terms of a philosophy of history. The master key to Vico's new science or metaphysics, as he says, was the discovery of the logic of poetic characters (*caratteri poetici*) or, as he also calls them, imaginative universals (*universali fantastici*).

Vico says that "the human mind is naturally impelled to take delight in uniformity" (NS 204). This desire for uniformity is manifested in the ages of gods and of heroes, in the ideal eternal history, in the form of fables that, Vico says, state ideal truths. He says, "So that, if we consider the matter well, poetic truth is metaphysical truth, and physical truth which is not in conformity with it should be considered false" (NS 205). Vico's example is the figure of Godfrey in Torquato Tasso's epic, *Jerusalem Delivered*. Godfrey is a poetic character formed by the imagination that defines a true chief of war, such that any potential chief of war who does not conform to the figure of Godfrey is not a true chief of war. Formulated in this way, it may appear that the poetic figure of Godfrey can be analogically predicated of individual chiefs. This is not Vico's point. The ideal figure of fables has "univocal, not analogical meanings for various particulars comprised under their poetic genera" (NS 210). Thus all particular individuals of which Godfrey is predicated are each literally Godfrey; they are not *like* Godfrey.

Vico has discovered a mode of thought or concept formation known to cultural anthropology and myth theory. The members of the Bear Clan

21. Cassirer, *Problem of Knowledge*, 296.

are all equally bears, and bears are them, and bears are bears. The clan members are not *like* bears. In poetic or what today would be called mythic thought, a particular functions as an imaginative universal. It is predicated of a class of particulars univocally, in the same way an abstract property is so predicated by rational mentality. For the poetic or mythic mind, unable to form the abstract concept of the virtue of courage embodied in the heroic figure of Achilles, any courageous individual *is* Achilles, and Achilles is Achilles. Such an individual is not *an* Achilles; Achilles is literally the being of the individual. Vico says that "the first men, the children, as it were, of the human race, not being able to form intelligible class concepts [*generi intelligibili*] of things, had a natural need to create poetic characters; that is, imaginative class concepts or universals, to which, as to certain models or ideal portraits, to reduce all the particular species which resembled them" (NS 209).

Vico realized that the intelligible class concepts of traditional logic, through which we construct our common-sense version of the world, presuppose a more concrete or immediate ordering of the world that occurs through the imagination or *fantasia*. As a term of Vico's metaphysics, *fantasia* may be understood as the "making imagination." It captures something of the meaning of the Greek *poiein*, to make and to compose poetry. The human world is first made through the power of *fantasia* and later through the power of ratiocination or *ragionamento*. Intelligible universals appear only in the third age. The mentality of ages of gods and heroes is formed through *fantasia*. The imaginative universals of the age of gods are concentrated on the formation of social institutions and natural phenomena. All of society and nature are full of gods. The imaginative universals of the age of heroes represent virtues that are required for society to have moral order.

Vico's imaginative universal is a new conception of metaphor. The conception of metaphor that derives from Aristotle's *Poetics* is the use of the name of one thing for another. A metaphor, thus, is a compact analogy. It is epistemic in nature because it depends upon our seeing one thing as like another, of projecting a similarity in dissimilars. It is an act that, as Aristotle says, cannot be taught and is a sign of genius. This sense of metaphor requires that the things to be likened to each other already have their own independent identities.

The imaginative universal is not an epistemological act, that is, an act of extending what is known into a new form. The imaginative universal is a metaphysical act, that is, an act of bringing a thing into existence. It is governed not by likeness but by identity. It brings what was not there before into existence. It does not extend what is already known in a further direction. The *ingenium* or *ingegno* involved in this metaphysical sense of metaphor is an aspect of memory, as described above in terms of Vico's threefold conception of memory. Metaphysics is an art of memory, as is this primordial sense of metaphor. *Ingenium* brings to mind what is already there in the memory. All that is in memory was originally in the senses, but it does not have an identity, a mental shape. *Fantasia*, joined with *ingegno*, makes the sensation remembered into an actuality. We will see this process at its purest in the formation of the imaginative universal of Jove that is the basis of poetic metaphysics. Jove is the archetype for all subsequent imaginative universals and is the first thought formed by the gentile peoples of Vico's ideal eternal history. Jove appears as the central figure of Vico's retelling of the biblical narrative.

Vico's story of humanity begins with the universal flood. The sons of Noah—Ham, Japeth, and Shem—and their offspring wander the great forests of the earth for two centuries, while the world dries out. They lose the religion of their father. They become *bestioni* and grow to the size of giants, becoming all body with little mind. The exception is a portion of the offspring of Shem that, after a century, is able to isolate itself and maintain the customs and laws of ancient Hebrew society, preserving its language and system of education. They also remain of normal stature. They, like the ancient Hebrews before the flood, have a direct relationship with God; they have a sacred history that does not undergo the three ages of the ideal eternal history of the gentile nations. The gentiles arise from the *giganti*, who have in their wandering lost the three principles of humanity—religion, marriage, and burial. The *giganti* live by their bodily strength, connected to their sensations and their passions.

A nation, for Vico, is a "birth" (*nascita*). His world of nations is not the modern political conception of nation-states. A nation is a *gens*, a people or number of families who have a common origin and are connected by a common descent and the use of the same gentile name. The world of gentile nations, for Vico, arises from the experience of Jove. As the earth becomes sufficiently dry the giants confront a new phenomenon: thunder and lightning in the sky. They perceive the sky as no higher than the tree-tops. The giants experience for the first time the feeling of terror (*spavento*). It is not an ordinary fear (*timore*) of a particular danger; it is a fear that comes over their whole being. It is the beginning of a first thought: they are, but they are not aware that they are. Only some of the giants respond in this way; they will become the fathers of the first families. In these giants, wonder is awakened. Vico says, "When wonder had been awakened in men by the first thunderbolts, these interjections of Jove should give birth to one produced by the human voice: *pa!*; and that this should then be doubled: *pape!*" (NS 448).

The first word is "Jove." Through their ability to utter this first word the noble giants make the first imaginative universal and produce a poetic metaphysics. Vico says that every gentile nation had its Jove. These giants have a double reaction to this experience: they imitate its sound and they flee into caves, out of sight of the sky, which is Jove's body. For those giants who are unable to form the thunder as Jove through the power of *fantasia*, thunder remains a series of immediate sensations, each being a unique object. Their mental abilities are active only at the level of sensation. As Vico says, for these proto-humans every facial expression was a new face.

The noble giants, however, can connect sensation to memory and connect one instance of thunder with another. They can find again, in successive moments, the same being as the first, and thus form the first name as a poetic character. This rise of Jove through fear is Vico's version of the biblical assertion that fear of the Lord is the beginning of wisdom—poetic wisdom. Language at this level is not articulate; it is bound up with gesture.

Cassirer, in his study of language as a symbolic form, points out that below any sense of articulate language, that is, language itself, are the two fundamental forms of the gesture. These two types of gesture exist side by side; one does not derive from the other. Cassirer holds that on one side we find the indicative (*die hinweisenden*) and on the other is the imitative (*die nachahmenden*) gesture. The indicative gesture or utterance is the act of pointing to what is meant, which is rooted in the primal act of grasping. This pointing is the first linguistic act: "For no animal progresses to the characteristic transformation of the grasping movement into the indicative gesture" (PSF 1:181). The indicative gesture is "clutching at a distance," which is distinctively human. The imitative gesture is as such distinctively human, but it is bound to the sense impression it attempts to duplicate. Cassirer says, "In imitation the I remains a prisoner of outward impression and its properties; the more accurately it repeats this impression, excluding all spontaneity of its own, the more fully the aim of the imitation has been realized" (PSF 1:182).

In describing the noble giants' reaction to the thunderous sky, Vico uses two precise verbs: *urlare* (to howl like an animal or shriek like a human) and *brontolare* (to rumble like thunder or grumble like a human). Vico says, "because in that state their nature was that of men all robust bodily strength, who expressed their very violent passions by shouting [*ur-lando*] and grumbling [*brontolando*], they pictured the sky to themselves as a great animated body, which in that aspect they called Jove, the first god of the so-called greater gentes, who meant to tell them something by the hiss of his bolts and the clap of his thunder" (*NS* 377). Their shouting is an indicative gesture that points to the being of the sky and causes them to flee into caves. Their grumbling is an imitative gesture that causes them to revere this new alter-body of the sky.

The first civilizing passion is fear, which leads to the second passion of civilized life—shame or modesty (*pudore*). For when they flee into caves they form the first marriages, out of the sight of Jove. These lead to the founding of the first families, who instigate the practice of burial. Burial establishes ancestors and lineage. Once the noble giants gain language they have what is distinctive to the human being and is the key to the human as social. As the first families make clearings in the great forests, which will eventually evolve into cities, they acquire divination to comprehend and worship the divine reality that is set over against their human being. Those giants who originally remain feral, still living in the forests, eventually seek protection with the fathers of the first families, and they become attached to these families as *famuli*, or indentured persons.

Thus human society, for Vico, from its beginnings comes about as an economic order based on a divine order of being. These first humans are theological poets who, through their *fantasia*, formulate a metaphysics that begins both the particular sciences, which originally take poetic form, and society, which also takes poetic form. Jove is the first apprehension of being. The first humans do not make Jove; they make a knowledge of Jove. And from this ability they make themselves as human. As their mind grows their great bodies, as Vico says, slowly return to normal size.

Providentiality

Jove is the first sign of God's providence, his relation to the world. Vico's aim is to conceive providence in history. In Latin, *providentia* and *prudentia* are synonyms. As providence, God is that ultimate reality whose sustaining power and ordering power provide continual guidance over the matters of human destiny. The providential order in human affairs is present as Vico's doctrine of ideal eternal history. Vico simply asserts the presence of providence in his metaphysics of history, but implicit in this assertion is a form of the teleological argument. Ideal eternal history, the patterns of the three ages of every nation's development seen through each nation's history, is a divine, not a human, order. History has a design that can be empirically substantiated and this design is followed by human beings in their making of history and in their making of a knowledge of history, but the design itself is not of human making.

Those interpreters who wish to regard Vico's new science as a doctrine of historicism are mistaken. They must ignore the presence of providence in it. It is with providence that Vico confronts what Mircea Eliade calls the "terror of history," the conception modern man has of man being the sole maker of history. As makers of history, human beings appear to command complete freedom. Yet this freedom has no beginning and no end. It is bereft of any trans-historical ground. The securing of a trans-historical ground requires the ability to repeat the origin. Vico's ontology of the appearance of Jove is primitive in that it is a repetition of the primitive ontology of the human need to return eternally to the beginning. Eliade says, "It could be said that this 'primitive' ontology has a Platonic structure; and in that case Plato could be regarded as the outstanding philosopher of 'primitive mentality,' that is, as the thinker who succeeded in giving philosophic currency and validity to the modes of life and behavior of archaic humanity."[22]

Vico's Neoplatonism brings ultimate being into history in the principle of ideal eternal history as a divine order of the human world that repeats itself. For Vico, each nation's historical life moves through the three ages of a *corso*. In this *corso*, "Men first feel necessity, then look for utility, next attend to comfort, still later amuse themselves with pleasure, thence grow dissolute in luxury, and finally go mad and waste their substance" (NS 241). The end of a *corso* is an ethical and rational madness, a barbarism of the intellect in which history becomes a nightmare from which no one can awake, and human beings, ceasing to have a relation to the trans-historical being of their own origin, finally *impazzano in istrappazzar le sostanze*. While pursuing luxury they have descended into a state comparable to the lowest region of Dante's *Inferno*, where the social fabric of human relations is eroded by cleverness and treachery.

When this stage occurs in a *corso*, Vico says, providence requires that humanity return to a new, primitive state, similar to its original state, in which human life is governed by necessities and a renewed awareness of religion. From this return there arises a *ricorso* of the three ages of gods,

22. Eliade, *Myth of the Eternal Return*, 34.

heroes, and humans. This *ricorso* is not a second *corso*, that is, a simple repetition of the first, because there is a memory of the first *corso*. God has failed to communicate to humanity the wisdom and piety that are necessary to preserve the institutions of religion, marriage, and burial. Human beings lose their fear of the divine; they cease to wonder and they become shameless, with no sense of virtue. The *ricorso* is a second attempt to convey these divine principles that govern society at its origin.

The *ricorso*, however, also ends in barbarism. It is a barbarism, Vico says, of *reflection* that develops over centuries, until humans are turned into "beasts made more inhuman by the barbarism of reflection [*la barbarie della riflessione*] than the first men had been made by the barbarism of sense [*la barbarie del senso*]" (NS 1106). Vico never speaks of *corsi e ricorsi*, as some commentators have said. He uses these terms only in the singular, not the plural. But since the providential God has not been able to communicate divine truth and virtue in the *ricorso*, it is conceivable that the *ricorso* could be followed by successive *ricorsi*.

Vico says, "But if the peoples are rotting in that ultimate civil disease and cannot agree on a monarch from within, and are not conquered and preserved by better nations from without, then providence for their extreme ill has its extreme remedy at hand" (NS 1106). This extreme remedy is the same as that enacted in the collapse of the *corso*. Vico says society will be returned "to the primitive simplicity of the first world of peoples, becoming again religious, truthful, and faithful. Thus providence brings back among them the piety, faith, and truth which are the natural foundations of justice as well as the graces and beauties of the eternal order of God" (NS 1106).

In the third age of the *corso* or the *ricorso*, human beings come to believe, in Eliade's terms, that they are the sole makers of history. As Eliade says, "For the modern man can be creative only insofar as he is historical; in other words, all creation is forbidden him except that which has its source in his own freedom; and, consequently, everything is denied him except the freedom to make history by making himself."[23] Here man is without human nature. Human beings are only their own activity that has no trans-historical limits. There is no human nature that is made by divine action on the basis of which human beings attain the freedom of their self-determination. Freedom is the negative concept of freedom from all limits. The terror that originally establishes the divine reality of Jove now becomes the terror of history, of historical making without any ultimate meaning.

23. Ibid., 156.

History becomes a scene of the matter in hand—all are busy with whatever project engages them. One project is as good as another. Such freedom is pure relativism. The meaning of anything is whatever it can be made to mean. All is permitted.

Although Vico claims his new science is dedicated to the glory of the Christian religion, his doctrine of providence as ideal eternal history is closer to paganism than to Christianity. History, for Vico, is not a drama of salvation, nor is it a doctrine of human progress. The truth that history repeats itself is expressed by the great Florentine historian, Francesco Guicciardini, who says, in his *Ricordi*: "All that which has been in the past and is at present will be again in the future. But both the names and the appearances of things change, so that he who does not have a good eye will not recognize them. Nor will he know how to grasp a norm of conduct or make a judgment by means of observation."[24] Guicciardini's "good eye" (*buono occhio*) is the key to understanding anything in human affairs and to understanding history itself.

Vico's *New Science* contains a new conception of prudence that differs from the classical conception of prudence as based on the study of the actions of great figures of the past. Vico's sense of prudence is based directly on a knowledge "of what providence has wrought in history," how "providence has ordered this great city of the human race" (NS 342). The great goal of philosophy is to teach us how to live. The fundamental requirement for this is prudence. Vico regards providence as a middle, a *to meson*, between what he calls the "blind chance" of Epicurus and the "deaf necessity" of the Stoics. Providential order allows for human choice and contingency of events, but these occur within an overall divine structure. This divine structure, when instituted at the human level, is law or *iurisprudentia*. The law, for Vico, is a complete system of civil wisdom. It is the true guide to human affairs. A legal case mirrors the interrelationship between the accidental or contingent aspects of events and the necessity the law provides to establish their meaning and worth. Providence is the application of the *ius gentium* to the life of nations. It is the "jurisprudence of the human race."

In the addition Vico wrote to the *New Science*, known as the *Pratica* or "practic" of the new science, he asserts a relation between contemplation or theoretical wisdom and prudence or practical wisdom. He says, "This entire work has so far been treated as a purely contemplative science concerning the common nature of nations. . . . It consequently seems to be

24. Guicciardini, *Ricordi*, 131. My translation.

lacking in the practic that all those sciences should have which are called 'active,' as dealing with matters that depend on human choice" (NS 1405). Vico says that the practic needed for human affairs can easily be derived from the contemplation of the providential order of the course of nations. He says, "Instructed by such contemplation, the wise men and princes of the republics will be able, through good institutions, laws, and examples, to recall the peoples to their *acme* or perfect state" (NS 1406). The *New Science* is a guide to good governance or political action that requires prudence, above all.

If we take Aristotle's view that ethics is part of politics (a part of the activity of persons in the *polis*), we can see that Vico's contemplative new science is a guide to prudence in individual actions. Prudent action in individual conduct requires attention both to what should be and what is. Any set of conditions has a course it will take, a beginning, middle, and end. Prudence requires the assessment of this particular course and the attempt to act successfully within its realities in terms of what should and can be. We can know the course of any set of conditions by the fact that everything in the human world repeats itself, as both Vico and Guicciardini assert. Memory, then, becomes the key to prudent action, and ingenuity, connected to it, allows us to find the similarities in the dissimilars necessary to guide our actions. The middle term between these two is imagination, which projects the possibilities in terms of which ingenuity can function.

If Vico's metaphysics of history provides a guide to our conception of moral philosophy, does it further provide a guide to the conduct of philosophy itself, its pursuit of wisdom? Philosophy appears in the ideal eternal history of a nation only when it enters its third age, its barbarism of the intellect. Vico's interpretation of Western history in terms of its *corso* and *ricorso* regards the age of gods and heroes to have occurred before Homer, who is a summary figure of them. The third age of the *corso* is the post-Homeric world of Greece and Rome that is distinguished by the invention of philosophy, which leads to forms of abstract thought, and luxury, in which the people finally waste their substance with the fall of Rome and the ancient world. Having been returned by providence to the necessities of life and the reinstitution of religion, the *ricorso* begins in what the Renaissance called the "dark ages," which develop to the heroic age of the high Middle Ages. These two ages are summarized by Dante, whom Vico calls the "Tuscan Homer."

With the Renaissance Humanists, philosophy appears again, this time by the revival of ancient philosophy that, as it develops into the modern period, produces the "barbarism of reflection," in which thought becomes abstract, divorced from its roots in *fantasia*. Law ceases to be the repository of civil wisdom and becomes a collection of claims of rights and the technical interpretation of them. Society becomes secular, with each individual opinion claiming to stand above any sense of authority, and life becomes the pursuit of wealth and luxury. It is said that Vico "looks at history and never smiles." No age is an intrinsically good age. The one point in ideal eternal history that is, perhaps, the best is that of the transition between the heroic and the creation of philosophy. This is the point of Socrates and of Platonic and Aristotelian philosophy in the ancient world of the *corso*, and of Pico della Mirandola and the Florentine Humanists in the *ricorso*. At this point the hero who embodied virtue has receded but is replaced by what Vico calls the "heroic mind" in his university oration of 1732.

Vico says, "'Hero' is defined by philosophers as one who seeks ever the sublime. Sublimity is, according to these same philosophers, the following, of the utmost greatness and worth: first, above nature, God Himself; next, within nature, this whole frame of marvels spread out before us, in which nothing exceeds man in greatness and nothing is of more worth than man's well-being, to which single goal each and every hero presses on, in singleness of heart."[25] Sublimity of thought is philosophy's dedication to a knowledge of the whole, of the three worlds of God, man, and nature. The two figures to whom Vico compares himself, in his autobiography, are Socrates and Pico della Mirandola.[26] The prudence of the philosopher is to cultivate the characteristics of the heroic mind. More cannot be done. In the age of the barbarism of reflection the philosopher's metaphysics of history is an art of memory that can teach the lessons of humane letters for any who can listen and learn.

25. Vico, "On the Heroic Mind," 230.
26. Vico, *Autobiography*, 156–57; 200.

5

The Infinity of the Absolute

The Mythology of Reason

AS MENTIONED IN CHAPTER 1, among Hegel's earliest works are the six
paragraphs known as "The Earliest System-Program of German Idealism,"
written approximately ten years before the *Phenomenology of Spirit* (1807).[1]
Hegel (1770–1831) says that he wishes to advance "an idea which, as far as
I know, has never occurred to anyone else—we must have a new mythology, but this mythology must be in the service of the ideas, it must be a
mythology of *Reason* [*Mythologie der Vernunft*]." Vico, in a single stroke in
the *New Science*, resolved the Platonic ancient "quarrel with the poets" by
making mythopoeic thought a form of wisdom that precedes philosophical
wisdom and is required by it as its starting point.

In the "System-Program" Hegel declares poetry to be the "instructress
of humanity [*die Leherin der Menscheit*]."[2] Hegel says his purpose in a philosophy of spirit (*Geist*) will be to make poetry in the end what it was in
the beginning. He says he wishes to take the idea of beauty in its Platonic
sense and that he is "now convinced that the highest act of reason, that in
which it embraces all ideas, is an aesthetic act." This aesthetic act of reason
is not intended by Hegel to reduce rational thought to poetry. It is instead
the claim that the idea is accessible only through the image. The imagination and reason cannot be separated. They are opposites that are required
of each other. The True that is the whole cannot be given a literal statement.

1. Hegel, "Das älteste Systemprogramm," 234–36.
2. Hegel makes the same point in the introduction to *Aesthetics*, 150.

Language can only take us to it. The access to the real requires an expanded conception of rationality that includes the immediacy of the image. In proper philosophical speech there is a dialectic between *Bild* (image) and *Begriff* (concept).

Hegel holds further that "the whole of metaphysics falls for the future within Morals [*die Moral*]" and that *Ethik* "will be nothing less than a complete system of all *Ideen*." The prime subject of metaphysics is the self as the agent of its own freedom. Metaphysics, even when it directs its attention to physics, is an activity of self-knowledge. How the self comes to know the world is part of how it comes to know itself. The self makes this knowledge of itself in speech. As the world is originally comprehended in mythopoeic terms, it is comprehended again in metaphysical terms. Metaphysical thinking, the thought of Ideas, includes the thought of their images. Or, as Hegel puts it, "The philosopher must possess just as much aesthetic power as the poet."

Hegel adds to these views in a fragment written prior to the *Phenomenology*, "Über Mythologie, Volkgeist und Kunst" (On mythology, "national spirit," and art).[3] In the "System-Program" he is concerned with how philosophy can be communicated to the people. He is aware that a people without a philosophy is a people without a culture. All peoples have mythologies but as rationality replaces them a way must be found for reason to enter national spirit. Myth lives through the image, and the mythic image survives through art. The question arises as to whether art can fully provide culture. Hegel's answer is that *Kunst* (art) and *Dichtkunst* (poetry) are not enough. They must be joined to *Vernunft* (reason) in order that human wisdom can be a whole. Thus in the "System-Program" he says, "Mythology must become philosophical in order to make the people rational [*vernünftig*], and philosophy must become mythological in order to make philosophers sensible [*sinnlich*]."

In holding this view I do not believe that Hegel is advocating philosophy for the masses. I think his position implicitly endorses the ancient threefold distinction of those who know, the refined (those who can come to know), and those who do not know—the hoi polloi who have no particular interest in knowledge, especially metaphysics. Philosophy requires a cultured society in order to exist. As Vico maintains, against Polybius,

---

3. This is one of a number of rediscovered Hegel manuscripts that Rosenkranz referred to in *Hegels Leben*. For a description of these manuscripts, see Ziesche, "Unbekannte Manuskripte," 430–44.

there cannot be a society composed simply of knowers or philosophers (NS 1110). Society requires a structure of images both of nature and of human nature to provide a medium through which its members can orient themselves and act.

In the *Volkgeist* fragment, Hegel says, "Mnemosyne, or the absolute Muse [*die absolute Muse*], art, assumes the aspect of presenting the externally perceivable, seeable, and hearable forms of spirit. This Muse is the generally expressed consciousness of a people. The work of art of mythology propagates itself in living tradition. As peoples grow in the liberation of their consciousness, so the mythological work of art continuously grows and clarifies and matures. This work of art is a general possession, the work of everyone. Each generation hands it down embellished to the one that follows; each works further toward the liberation of absolute consciousness."[4]

The "mythological work of art" is what today would simply be called myth, in the sense that Cassirer understands "mythical thought" as a symbolic form, the total thought form that lies at the beginning of human culture, with its own versions of cause, object, space, time, number, and self. These correspond to Vico's "poetic wisdom." Art is a separate symbolic form that develops as a counterpart to "language" understood as a symbolic form in which the world is grasped not in images but in terms of classes of objects to which words refer. Cassirer says, "Like all the other symbolic forms art is not the mere reproduction of a ready-made, given reality. It is one of the ways leading to an objective view of things and of human life."[5]

Cassirer says that "myth, language and art begin as a concrete, undivided unity, which is only gradually resolved into a triad of independent modes of spiritual creativity."[6] Through art the image achieves a purely "aesthetic" function. Language, having realized its discursive and classificative power, becomes a means of artistic expression. Cassirer says, "Here it recovers the fullness of life; but it is no longer a life mythically bound and fettered, but an aesthetically liberated life. . . . This liberation is achieved not because the mind throws aside the sensuous forms of word and image, but in that it uses them both as organs of its own, and thereby recognizes them for what they really are: forms of its own self-revelation."[7] Both Hegel and Cassirer see freedom as a process of self-determination. Hegel recognizes

---

4. For a translation of this complete passage, see Verene, *Hegel's Recollection*, 36–37.

5. Cassirer, *Essay on Man*, 143.

6. Cassirer, *Language and Myth*, 98.

7. Ibid., 98–99.

that in the liberation of consciousness from the "mythological work of art" there is also a loss. Hegel regards the individual artist not as a creator of novelty but as an agent of *Volkgeist*. What the artist creates grows from the consciousness of a people, and in that sense it is mythic. The artwork is an expression of a peoples' self-identity. Hegel says, "There is always one who brings it [the artwork] to its final completion by being the last to work on it and he is the darling of Mnemosyne."[8]

The power that myth has to have for its images to provide exclusive access to the real—to society, nature, and the gods—is not reproduced in art, which is a form existing alongside commonsensical and scientific orders of experience. Hegel says, "When in our time the living world does not form the work of art within it, the artist must place his imagination in a past world; he must dream a world, but the character of dreaming, of not being alive, of the past, is plainly stamped on his work."[9] This is an early statement of Hegel's famous thesis of the death of art that he announces in the introduction and conclusion of his *Lectures on Fine Art*. In these lectures Hegel claims that with the development of the romantic art of emotion, art no longer unites itself with anything objective. Art becomes an expression of the subjective world of emotions and feelings. The romantic pursuit of art results in the standpoint of comedy, in which the subject can confront its own reality solely through the conditions it itself creates. Hegel says, "On this peak comedy leads at the same time to the dissolution [*Auflösung*] of art altogether."[10] Because of this development of art in terms of emotion into comedy, art, Hegel says, has ceased to be the highest need of *Geist*. Hegel says art "remains for us a thing of the past."[11]

The self-assured, subjective, aesthetic personality of the artist is not the agent of *Volkgeist* and the darling of Mnemosyne. It cancels everything not correspondent with itself. The artist and the artwork become purely particular. Hegel's claim of the end of art is not that artists will stop producing works of art but rather that *Geist* in its form as art reaches a limit. To obtain the object again, consciousness must pass to religion, in which thought takes place in *Vorstellungen* or "picture-thinking," and then on to philosophy. Philosophy, like myth, forms reality in categorical terms, not in hypothetical terms. In its subjectivity, art offers various "hypothetical"

8. See Verene, *Hegel's Recollection*, 37.

9. Ibid.

10. Hegel, *Aesthetics*, 2:1236.

11. Ibid., 1:25.

portraits of human nature and the world. Philosophy's aim is to present the "really real." Its mode of thinking must reactivate the mythic power of the image without returning thought to myth itself. The mythic world, once lost, can be reached only by memory. Thus Hegel's view agrees with Vico's, that "memory is imagination." Philosophy must regard reason as having imagination as its double. *Bild* cannot be divorced from *Begriff*. This is what Hegel means by the need for a "mythology of reason." Hegel makes poetry a part of philosophy.

Hegel achieves this doubleness in his *Phenomenology of Spirit*, which he regards as his introduction to metaphysics. At the end of the work he characterizes the whole of it as a *Gallerie von Bildern*, a "gallery of images." Hegel's text is stylistically a dialectic between *begriffliches Denken* and *bildhaftes Denken*. Each offers access to the other. Once we have read its text we recall to mind its meaning through its unforgettable images—*die sinnliche Gewissheit* (sense certainty), *Herrschaft und Knechtschaft* (master and servant), *die verkehrte Welt* (the inverted world), *das unglückliche Bewusstsein* (the unhappy or unfortunate consciousness), *Schädellehre* (the doctrine of the phrenological skull), *das geistige Tierreich* (the spiritual zoo or menagerie), *die absolute Freiheit und der Schrecken* (absolute freedom and terror), *die schöne Seele* (the beautiful soul), and so forth. Hegel also uses specific metaphors, in addition to those that function as headings for sections of the text, e.g., *die Arbeit des Negativen* (the labor of the negative), *die List der Vernunft* (the cunning of reason), and the night in which all cows are black (*alle Kühe Schwarz sind*). This last ironic metaphor, with complete efficiency, dismisses all idealist metaphysics based on a dialectic of the identity of opposites such that the Absolute is nothing but A = A.

These images are the master key to Hegel's *Phenomenology* or "science of the experience of consciousness." They teach us how to approach the text, how to join our imagination to reason, and move through the stages of consciousness. If we become lost in the conceptual structure of a stage, they bring us back to re-enter it. The ability to think truly philosophically requires the power of the metaphor. The metaphor supplies the beginning point for reason. It is the threshold through which we pass to think the idea. The idea is reached by allowing the ingenuity that generates the metaphor to pass on to the question. Hegel's dialectic moves forward in consciousness by each stage coming to question itself, thus seeking a new beginning.

Hegel's solution to the ancient quarrel is to acknowledge the wisdom of the poets and to set poetry in motion as the teacher of speculative reason, because poetry is originally the teacher of all humanity. But the lessons so learned are on reason's terms. Reason commands the dialectic of question and answer that develops within consciousness. It controls the images of the poets through its commitment to the logic of the idea. This dialectic, however, takes the subjective beyond itself and produces self-knowledge as an objective process in which the subjective self transforms itself into *Geist*.

When the phenomenology of spirit which leads to metaphysics (Hegel's *Science of Logic*) comes on the scene, it is the end of art, for art cannot sustain itself apart from its natural dialectic with philosophy. It is only through this dialectic that great art can have meaning. Art, which, as mythology, once maintained itself in the living tradition, in our time is alive only through its attachment to speculative reason. The extent to which art, like philosophy, takes spirit toward the Absolute, is the extent to which art attains to an objective truth. It takes us to a vision of the whole. Otherwise its creations remain simply novelties of subjectivity.

The Dialectic of the Double *Ansich*

The first book to be written in English on Hegel's philosophy was *The Secret of Hegel* (1865), by James Hutchison Stirling, the first appointed Gifford lecturer at Edinburgh. Stirling says, "Yes, there is a secret, and every man feels it, and every man asks for the key to it—every man who approaches even so near as to look at this mysterious and inexplicable labyrinth of Hegel. Where does it begin, we ask, and how did it get this beginning, and what unheard of thing is this which is offered us as the clue with which we are to guide ourselves?"[12] Stirling's revelation of the secret requires 750 pages, including a translation of the first three chapters of the *Science of Logic* and commentary on them.

Stirling says, "The secret of Hegel may be indicated at shortest thus: As Aristotle—with considerable assistance from Plato—made *explicit* the *abstract* Universal that was *implicit* in Socrates, so Hegel—with less considerable assistance from Fichte and Schelling—made *explicit* the *concrete* Universal that was *implicit* in Kant."[13] The secret of Hegel was his recovery of Reason from its displacement from the center of philosophy by the Understanding in Kantian critique and its replacement as the highest achievement of thought. Stirling says, "We can conceive now how Hegel was

12. Stirling, *Secret of Hegel*, 81.
13. Ibid., xxii.

enabled to get beyond the limited subjective form of Kant's mere system of human knowledge, and convert that system into something universal and objective. The thing-in-itself had disappeared, individuals had disappeared; there remained only an absolute, and this absolute was named Reason."[14]

Stirling's approach to the relations between Kant's idealism and Hegel's is a breath of fresh air. He understands German philosophy to be a continuous development, as he also sees ancient Greek philosophy to be. In my experience among today's Kant scholars, they regard Kantian critique as an acme of philosophical thought and join this with a position of anti-Hegelianism. Against this provincial view, the history of philosophy shows that idealism is a continuous development through which philosophy itself moves from Kant to Hegel and beyond. The subjective idealism of Kant should be given its due, but how foolish to keep harping on the correctness of Kantian philosophy, when it is absorbed by Hegel and idealism itself is advanced thereby. Hegelians, at least in large part, in my experience, do not regard Hegel's thought as the be-all and end-all of philosophy but as a most fruitful position from which to take philosophy further. As Hegel would insist, it is the True itself that counts. Every philosophy is a child of its time, but philosophy itself, the wisdom of the whole, is transhistorical.

If the secret of Hegel is the concrete universal, the *Begriff*, the key to this universal is its dialectical existence. One of the great misreadings in the history of philosophy is the legend that Hegel's dialectic is a process of thesis-antithesis-synthesis. This legend has been definitively debunked in an article by Gustav Mueller, "The Hegel Legend of 'Thesis-Antithesis-Synthesis.'" Mueller thinks that this description of Hegel's dialectical method has arisen because of difficulties in comprehending Hegel's terminology generally. He says, "These linguistic troubles, in turn, have given rise to legends which are like perverse and magic spectacles—once you wear them, the text simply vanishes."[15] Hegel's terminology is no more technical than that of Socrates. Hegel takes words of ordinary German speech and invests them with systematic meanings. In his well-known letter to Voss, the translator of Homer, of May 1805, Hegel writes, "Luther made the Bible, you have made Homer speak German—the greatest gift that can be made to a people . . . of my own effort, I wish to say that I will attempt to teach philosophy to speak German."[16]

14. Ibid., 89.
15. Mueller, "Hegel Legend," 411.
16. Hegel to Johann Heinrich Voss, in *Briefe*, 1:99–100. My translation.

Hegel's task is more difficult than that of Luther or Voss, who are translating from one language to another. Hegel must get his reader to grasp the German language in a new way. In so doing it is all too easy for the reader to bring, into Hegel's new meanings, old meanings that are familiar. It is an example of Vico's second axiom: "It is another property of the human mind that whenever men can form no idea of distant and unknown things, they judge them by what is familiar and at hand" (NS 122). Glockner's *Hegel-Lexicon* shows that Hegel never uses the combination of thesis-antithesis-synthesis to describe his own philosophy, as does the *Register* of the Suhrkamp edition of Hegel's *Werke*. Hegel speaks of the triadic method of thought in two places. In both he attributes it to Kantian philosophy. In the preface to the *Phenomenology* he criticizes *Triplizität*, which he identifies with the abstract formalism of Kantian thinking (PS 50; 41), and in his lectures on the *History of Philosophy* he mentions this triplicity of Kant and calls it a *geistloses Schema*.[17]

How did this legend begin, if not from Hegel himself? Mueller discovered that in the winter of 1835–36, about four years after Hegel's death, a group of Kantians in Dresden asked Heinrich Mortiz Chalybäus, a professor of philosophy at Kiel, to lecture on the new idealism. They wished the new philosophy of Hegelianism to be a confirmation of their own Kantianism. The lectures of Chalybäus, which were published as a book a year later and circulated in three editions, characterized Hegel's method in terms of thesis-antithesis-synthesis, projecting this triplicity on to the first three sections of the first chapter of Hegel's *Science of Logic*—being, nothing, and becoming. These three sections could appear to be a metaphysical triplicity, corresponding to any of Kant's epistemological triplicities, such as the schematism of the understanding that synthesizes the concept and the sensible intuition.

The thesis-antithesis-synthesis theory of Hegel's method is furthered by the fact that Hegel's *Encyclopedia of the Philosophical Sciences in Outline* is in three parts and its divisions are organized in threes. But this is a textbook whose divisions are superficial to the subject matter itself. Hegel warns, in the preface to the *Phenomenology*, against a "table of contents" mentality, which he says is all the Understanding brings. It is not the mentality of Reason, which has no such static divisions in its self-development. George Kline, in an article written some years ago on Hegel literature in various languages, notes that modern scholarship has made little or no use

---

17. See Mueller's comment in "Hegel Legend," 412.

of this threefold division.[18]Among English-language interpreters of Hegel's thought only W. T. Stace wears Mueller's magic spectacles. It is significant that Stace approaches Hegel's system only through the divisions of the *Encyclopedia*.[19]

If Hegel's dialectical method is not a triplicity of three movements, what is it? Hegel's answer, for the reader, is ready at hand. He explains his dialectic at the beginning of his system, in the several introductory pages of the *Phenomenology*, the work he conceived as the first part of his system, the second of which is the *Science of Logic*, his metaphysics. Hegel's dialectic is a logic of *coincidentia oppositorum*, what was discovered by Cusanus and Bruno as an ontological and cosmological principle. Hegel transforms this into a phenomenological principle that offers us a science of consciousness that is the prerequisite for a science of being. Hegel's dialectic is a two-step, not a three-step, process. There is no moment of synthesis in which the two fundamental moments of consciousness—the object as in-itself (*Ansich*) and the object as for consciousness (*Fürsich*)—are united. Consciousness always finds itself on one side of itself or another in the apprehension of its object.

There are two passages in which Hegel states, with complete directness, the points upon which his phenomenological method rests. He says, "But the distinction between the in-itself and knowledge is already present in the very fact that consciousness knows an object at all. Something is *for it* the *in-itself*; and knowledge, or the being of the object for consciousness, is, *for it*, another moment. Upon this distinction, which is present as a fact, the examination rests" (PS 85; 72). So there can be no mistaking Hegel's clarity here, the final sentence of this quotation is: "*Auf dieser Unterscheidung, welche vorhanden ist, beruht die Prüfung.*" This is Hegel's discovery: that there are two moments of consciousness, neither of which can be in any sense or manner reduced to the other. Neither is the ground of the other. These are two senses of the in-itself, the *Ansich*, so that each requires the other. To put it simply, there is (*a*) a consciousness of something, and (*b*) a consciousness which is the consciousness of the consciousness of the object.

The connection between these two moments *is not a relation*, but these two moments are necessary aspects of each other. This necessity is what any relation attempts specifically to form. They make all relations in

---

18. Kline, "Reinterpretations of Hegel's Philosophy," 46–47.

19. Stace, *Philosophy of Hegel*.

experience possible. Their necessity is not a relation. The illusion each stage of the development of consciousness has is that it can bridge the absolute difference between these two moments, by some principle of relation, and thus synthesize them. Every shape consciousness takes relies on these two distinct yet inseparable moments. For consciousness to pass from the first moment to the second is what Hegel means by experience (*Erfahrung*).

Experience is this doubled *Ansich*. Consciousness travels within itself (*fahren, erfahren*) in terms of the coincidence of these two moments. The doubled *Ansich* is the *dialektische Bewegung*, dialectical movement. Once the initial moment of *Ansich* is taken up as an object for consciousness, *Für-sich*, it is another *Ansich*, but it is now an *Ansich* realized by consciousness. To apprehend this second *Ansich* as being for consciousness, consciousness must take another step back, so to speak, and realize it as an object for itself, and so forth. Consciousness seeks, through its self-movement, to have these two moments reunited. Hegel says, "But the goal is as necessarily fixed for knowledge as the serial progression; it is the point where knowledge no longer needs to go beyond itself, where knowledge finds itself, where concept [*Begriff*] corresponds to object and object to concept" (PS 80; 69). The end of this sentence reads, "*der Begriff dem Gegenstande, der Gegenstand dem Begriffe entspricht.*"

Entsprechen has the sense of answering, suiting, matching, being in accord with, meeting with, or corresponding. The highest state of knowing, the goal that consciousness seeks, is not available as a *unification, synthesis,* or *identification* of concept and object. The term *entsprechen* preserves the notion of speaking, *sprechen,* and adds the prefix *ent-*. This prefix, understood purely in philosophical terms, designates the idea of entering into a new state, or the abandonment of an old. These two, the object and the concept, attain at the point of absolute knowing a kind of corresponding to each other. In the last sentence of these pages of his introduction to the *Phenomenology,* Hegel says that when consciousness reaches its goal of absolute knowing, it arrives at a point where "*die Erscheinung dem Wesen gleich wird,*" where the appearance and essence become *gleich* (PS 89; 75). He does not say they become identical or unified, but *gleich*—the same, like, equal, equivalent, alike, similar, resembling, or proportionate. They do not merge into one. Their opposition coincides.

In explaining this point, Hegel says further, "It shows up here like this: since what first appeared as the object sinks for consciousness to the level of its way of knowing it, and since the in-itself becomes a *being-for-consciousness* of the in-itself, the latter is now the new object. Herewith a new pattern of consciousness comes on the scene as well, for which the essence is something different from what it was at the preceding stage. It is this fact that guides the entire series of the patterns of consciousness in their necessary sequence" (PS 87; 73–74).

In the grasp of the two levels of *Ansich*—consciousness of the object and consciousness of the object for consciousness—the root meaning of necessity is grasped. The motion of the second sense of the *Ansich* entails that it become a being-for-consciousness: "das *Ansich* zu einem *Für-das-Bewusstsein-Sein des Ansich wird*." Hegel does not declare this new object to be in any sense a synthesis. He does not even call it a being in-and-for-itself (an *An-und-für-sich Sein*). He calls it a *Für-das-Bewusstsein-Sein des Ansich*—"a for consciousness being of the in-itself." This consciousness is a new birth of the object, an *Entstehung*, a new standing. It is no mere repeat of the original *Ansich*, because it is the result of it. Every move consciousness makes in the knowing of its object is a reaffirmation of the original two moments of the *doubled Ansich*. As consciousness continues to grasp the ever-changing object for itself, it slowly realizes that the object is not a true or independent other but an opposite of itself that is in fact itself in an ever-changing garb. The science of the experience of consciousness is a science of opposites that is self-knowledge. What consciousness knows is itself.

True Infinity

In the *Encyclopedia Logic*, Hegel says that "the true infinite [*das wahrhafte Unendliche*]" is the "fundamental concept of philosophy [*der Grundbegriff der Philosophie*]."[20] All metaphysics depends upon the proper comprehension of the concept of infinity. In metaphysics we encounter all that is fundamental in philosophy, that on which the rest of philosophy depends. Without metaphysics there is no philosophy, there is only a general form of critical thinking, taken to this subject or another.

Infinity is the essence of the being of God. God's essence and existence are identical. The world's essence and its existence are finite but not identical. The being of the world is finite because it is limited. The limits are opposites governed by the opposition between essence and existence. The finitude of the world raises the question of its relation to the infinite being of God. Infinity is the most important concept for philosophy, since the

20. Hegel, *Logic of Hegel: Encyclopaedia*, 179 (sec. 95).

name for God, in conceptual terms, is the Absolute. To discover the true concept of infinity is to give form to the assertion of the ontological argument of God as the being of which none greater can be conceived. God's infinity cannot be conceived as simply a divine property, or God's essence and existence would be opposites. They would not coincide.

In like manner, God's infinity, or, in philosophical terms, the infinity of the Absolute, cannot be conceived as the opposite of the world's finitude, or God would simply exist as an opposite to creation and as an opposite not different in principle from what is created. The solution to this problem is what Cusanus sought, in his theory of the infinite line, as the conception of the *coincidentia oppositorum* that is taken up by Bruno in his doctrine of the infinite universe and worlds.

Cusanus and Bruno offer us the correct statement of the problem but are unable to complete its solution. They are held back by the concept of substance and by the lack of a self-developing dialectic. In the *Phenomenology*, Hegel demonstrates how substance becomes subject (PS 17; 19). Substance metaphysics comprehends the object as a thing in which properties inhere. The object has no internal life. When substance is reconceived as subject, by Hegel, its being is characterized by an internal dialectic through which it becomes what it is. Bruno approaches this sense of the object with his cosmology of the infinite worlds, each being like an animal.

Hegel distinguishes between "bad-infinite" (*Schlecht-Unendliche*) and the "true infinite" (*wahrhaftes Unendliche*). The bad infinite is infinity conceived as the simple opposite of the finite. As the opposite to the finite, the bad infinite is a progression or series that simply goes on and on, without end. But it is also not a true concept of the unlimited because it is only intelligible as opposite to the finite. The true infinite is a dialectical movement in which the whole systematically recapitulates itself. Hegel speaks of this in the *Phenomenology*, but the *locus classicus* for his discussion of infinity is in the second chapter on existence in the *Science of Logic*. In the *Phenomenology* Hegel discusses bad infinity in relation to the presence of the supersensible world in the "inverted world of Force and Understanding," and the bad infinity typifies the inability of consciousness to unite itself in the "unhappy consciousness." Hegel also uses the term "bad infinity" in his criticism of physiognomy in his stage of "observing reason" (PS 322; 236).

Hegel's concept of the true infinity can best be grasped by following through his primary account of it in the *Science of Logic* as he generates the true from the bad infinity. Hegel says, "It is essential to distinguish the true concept of infinity from bad infinity, the infinite of reason from the infinite of the understanding. The latter is in fact a *finitized* infinite, and, as we shall now discover, in wanting to maintain the infinite pure and distant from the finite, the infinite is by that very fact only made finite" (SL 109; 1:125).

The understanding functions only in terms of reflective thinking. The knowing subject determines its object by making static distinctions through which it apprehends the object. Thus the understanding can grasp the difference between the finite and the infinite only as a pure difference. In so doing the infinite cannot be realized except as an opposite of the finite, and is nothing more than a "finitized infinite." The understanding cannot rise to the level of speculative thinking; that is the province of reason. Reason regards the opposition of knowing subject and object known as dynamic, a progression of dialectical development in which each determinate moment of opposition is finite but which itself is infinite. To think in this manner is closed to the understanding's prison house of reflection, and it cannot reach beyond bad infinity.

In the understanding, the infinite is "burdened with the opposition to the finite, and this finite, as an other, remains a real existence. . . . Contrasted with the finite, with the series of existent determinacies, of realities, the infinite is indeterminate emptiness, the beyond of the finite, whose being-in-itself is not in its existence (which is something determinate)" (SL 110–11; 1:127–28). The infinite of the understanding is a pure beyond, a *Jenseits*, with no power of internal determination. It is bereft of any sense of self-identity. It is something, but because of its indeterminateness its being is equivalent to nothing, an abstraction of the understanding without content. At this point we can clearly see why the understanding is incapable of metaphysics. At best the understanding can organize the contents of experience but can provide no ground except for the subject's principles of its own knowing.

Hegel continues, "As thus posited over against the finite, the two connected by the qualitative mutual reference of *others*, the infinite is to be called the *bad infinite*, the infinite of the *understanding*, for which it counts as the highest, the absolute truth. The understanding believes that it has attained satisfaction in the reconciliation of truth while it is in fact entangled in unreconciled, unresolved, absolute contradictions" (SL 111; 1:128). The bad infinite is a dead end for thought. Unable to approach the real, thought retreats into itself to formulate transcendental truths. The understanding can find no route to the transcendent and so must dismiss it as a propensity thought has to pursue illusions.

The true infinity arises out of the bad infinity by the dialectical transcendence of their doubleness of each other: "Each is equally only a moment of the other. Since both, the finite and the infinite, are themselves moments of the progress, they are *jointly the finite,* and since they are equally jointly negated in it and in the result, this result as the negation of their joint finitude is called with truth the infinite. Their distinction is thus the *double meaning* which they both have" (SL 118, 1:137).

Once the opposition of the finite and the infinite of the bad infinity attempt to define each other in terms of their opposition, the true infinite begins to emerge. They become determinate moments in an infinite progression that is a simple series of steps into the beyond, but in a self-limiting movement in which each moment in the progression is completely determinate but the progression itself is unlimited. This sense of self-determination is the metaphysical ground for Hegel's claim that freedom is self-determination.

Hegel concludes, "The claim that the *finite is an idealization* defines *idealism.* The idealism of philosophy consists in nothing else than the recognition that the finite is not truly an existent. Every philosophy is essentially idealism or at least has idealism for its principle, and the question then is only how far this principle is carried out. This applies to philosophy just as much as to religion, for religion also, no less than philosophy, will not admit finitude as a true being, an ultimate, an absolute, or as something non-posited, uncreated, eternal" (SL 124; 1:145). For religion as for philosophical idealism, the infinite is present in the finite. The finite is not as such existent. It is existent only in its realization in the infinite, which is the ever-present reality of all that there is.

Hegel says that the proper image of the true infinite is not a straight line. He says, "As true infinite, bent back upon itself, its image becomes the *circle,* the line that has reached itself, closed and wholly present, without *beginning* and *end*" (SL 119; 138–39). This comment on the straight line and circle might be considered as a reference to Cusanus's use of the straight line to symbolize his conception of the infinite that approaches but does not reach Hegel's concept of the true infinity. Yet there is curiously no reference to Cusanus in any of Hegel's works, including his comments on late medieval into modern philosophy in his *Lectures on the History of Philosophy.* It is especially curious since Cusanus is the beginning both of

German philosophy and of modern philosophy, and editions of his writings were known and available in Hegel's time.

The circle is Hegel's figure. He calls his whole "system of science" a circle and in fact he says it is a circle of circles (*ein Kreis von Kreisen*), so that each member returns to its own beginning and is the beginning of the next member. Hegel says, at the end of the *Science of Logic*, that each one of the sciences in his system of science is joined to the others as links in a chain (*Kette*). Thus, "Fragments of this chain are the single sciences, each of which has a *before* and an *after*—or, more accurately said, *has in possession* only the *before* and in its conclusion *points to its after*" (SL 751–52; 2:504).

This is not the sense of a circle in which once the series of links are linked to themselves the circle becomes a hoop—a smooth, self-enclosed structure. The sense of links remains. The moments are *linked* to each other; what is in-itself is *linked* (is *entspreched*) to what is for-itself. Links touch where one ends and the other, so to speak, begins. Links are not continuous. There is a "gap." This gap is as much a part of what makes the chain a chain, but it is as such never a "moment" in the chain and it never becomes one of its links. This gap is always absolutely present.

In characterizing the connection between the two moments of the double *Ansich*, Hegel uses the formulation of *Anundfürsichsein*, being in and for itself (e.g., PS 25; 24). He never writes *Anfürsichsein*. The "and" (*das Und*) is always the term that joins these two senses of being. In the *Science of Logic*, in describing the finite and infinite as opposites, Hegel says each refers to its other: "Taken *without this connecting reference* [that they are others of each other], and thus joined only through an 'and,' they subsist independently, each only an existent over against the other" (SL 114; 1:132).

The "and" is the perpetual gap within the being of consciousness, since consciousness regains the opposition of in-itself and the for-itself in order to have experience. The "and" is the placeholder of their difference, their mutual necessity that is not convertible into a particular relation, but this convertibility is continually attempted by consciousness in the stages of its self-development, each of which produces only an illusion of the resolution of their opposition.

The *Phenomenology* is a *Narrenschiff*—a ship of fools—for each of its stages is a type of folly. It is a book of irony, the irony of human existence. Things are never what they seem. Once the stage of absolute knowing is reached, consciousness is ready to go forth as rational thought, free of the illusion that the two fundamental moments of consciousness can in fact be resolved into each other. No such realization is possible as an experience in which the concept is brought together with the sense perception.

The *Science of Logic* originates from the question as to whether the resolution of opposites can be *thought*, be accomplished at the level of the idea. Consciousness become thought has attained the wisdom that it may freely attempt to think the "and." The attempt by reason to freely think the two sides of the opposition as one, to overcome the coincidence of contraries, is what drives forward the progression of stages of the *Logic*. Opposition is first thought as being, the first stage of the *Logic*, because both sides of an opposition joined by the "and" are. Both have being. But being is quickly shown to be no more than something that is indeterminate. Being can be affirmed of anything. In its indeterminacy it is thus equivalent to nothing. The movement from being to nothing produces becoming and so forth, each thought being an idea that attempts to overcome the "and" until the absolute idea is resolved. Unlike the progression of consciousness, thought in its progression of categories is not under any illusion. It is secure in the wisdom that it is only systematically assembling thought as thought.

At the moment of the absolute idea, Hegel says that the idea now goes forth "freely as nature." This claim has been a classic part of criticism of Hegel's idealism, reflecting the general criticism of idealism that the real is not solely determined by ideas. Seen from the perspective developed here, Hegel's comment is quite harmless. It in no sense alleges that nature will be deduced from the idea. The idea can freely go forth as nature because consciousness has already freely gone forth as thought, as the idea, as the absolute knowing of the *Phenomenology* goes forth to become the absolute idea, the thought of the *Logic*. As the oppositions of each of the stages of Hegel's dialectic are held together by "and," so all the parts of his system are linked by "and." The idea simply finds nature as its opposite.

Absolute Knowing

Absolutes Wissen is the final stage of the *Phenomenology*. It is doctrine of wisdom, for wisdom is a knowledge of the whole. To read the *Phenomenology* as a dialectical progression of thesis-antithesis-synthesis is to see this progression as analogous to rolling a great snowball. Each stage is synthesized into the next until all the stages, progressively rolled together with each other, reach the final stage of absolute knowing that contains them all, as the snowball, with each push, increases to greater and greater size.

This is the snowball theory of the Absolute. It is as far from visualizing the meaning of Hegel's assertion that the "True is the whole" and the role of absolute knowing in establishing it as one can get. The content of one stage of consciousness is not incorporated into the next. The movement from one stage to another is a transformation of how the object is formed. Hegel says that consciousness constantly forgets how it arrived at a given point, and must begin again, and then *"fängt die Bewegung von vorne an"* (PS 109; 86). This process of *aufheben* has a sense of irony about it.

The thesis-antithesis-synthesis theory and the snowball theory both fail to comprehend Hegel's conception of *aufheben*. *Aufheben* is a verb used in ordinary German that has no genuine equivalent in English. It has often been rendered as "supersede" and as "sublate." *Aufheben* is Hegel's term for the way in which one stage of consciousness is transformed into a succeed-ing stage, the sense in which a preceding stage is replaced yet absorbed into and incorporated in a new way into a succeeding stage. A basic metaphor for this sense of progress is the way in which, within the consciousness of any human being, the world of the child is transformed by stages into the world of the adult. The adult is the product of childhood, but in the adult the childishness of the child is canceled, while something of the personality formed in childhood is preserved.

Aufheben is not a mysterious or technical term. It is a part of ordinary German conversation, as are more or less all of Hegel's terms. It has four basic meanings, and Hegel exploits them all at once to convey his dialectic. *Aufheben* can mean (1) to lift or raise something up, as in the simple sense of the verb *heben*, "to raise"; (2) to take something up, to pick it up or even to seize it in an active sense (*heben* intensified by *auf*); (3) to keep or pre-serve something, to retain it; and (4) to abolish, annul, cancel, or put an end to something. In ordinary speech, *aufheben* can be used to emphasize one or more of these four senses. Readers of Hegel have often made too much of this term. The process of development that Hegel is presenting with this term is certainly known to the English speaker, but the concept of it cannot be expressed in a single, transitive verb. Hegel is well aware, with his use of *aufheben* as a lay term for his dialectic, or with other terms of his philoso-phy, that he is having philosophy speak German. He defines what he means by this term in his stage of "Perception" in the *Phenomenology* (PS 113; 90).

Aufheben may be understood in relation to the Latin term *ingenium*, similar to but differing, to an extent, from the English "ingenuity." Ingenuity or *ingenium* is not a method in a Cartesian sense. It is the way consciousness or thought accomplishes what it needs to accomplish in any given moment. *Ingenium* has the sense of perception of connection between what is diverse. This perception can result in a metaphor on the one hand or in an intellectual hypothesis on the other. *Ingenium* is the talent of the mind to be inventive. It is a response to what is immediately before the mind that is needed. The mind must simply, on the basis of its present state, take itself to a further state, one that has never been for it before. *Ingenium*, as we have seen in Vico's definition, is a part of memory. To produce a new perception of the connection between things, *ingenium* requires memory. Memory is the storehouse of *ars topica*, of connections that can suggest what is needed for thought or consciousness to advance. The answer to skepticism is in this sense of ingenuity. Skepticism, as Hegel says, just throws things into the same empty abyss with its constant practice of doubt (PS 79; 68).

On the last page—the last paragraph—of the *Phenomenology*, Hegel calls forth the absolute Muse. He calls forth the Muse four times, that is, he uses *Erinnerung* four times. He waits until the final moment to give a name to that power of consciousness by which consciousness can have a speculative knowledge of its own activity. Here Hegel says that the forms of spirit in their contingency and history, taken together with their conceptual organization, are conceptual history or recollection. *Erinnerung*, which can be translated by the English word "recollection" but which does not preserve the sense of "inner," *das Innere*, is the master key to the *Phenomenology*.

Hegel's work is a colossus of systematic memory. This science cannot be reached by reflection, which is unable to penetrate the inner being of things. It can be reached only by recollection. The reflective sentence merely names and classifies things. The speculative sentence, *spekulativer Satz* (PS 61; 51), takes us inside the object dialectically, taking the meaning of the subject into the predicate and then taking the subjectified predicate back into the subject, transforming it into a new state of its meaning.

In Hegel's second use of *Erinnerung* he hyphenates it as *Er-Innerung*. Ernst Bloch, in a lecture on language and culture, remarked, "In Hegel's *Phenomenology* one notices quite frequently how a sudden linguistic insight is inextricably bound up with true philosophical invention. This occurs when Hegel separates the word re-collection [*Er-Innerung*] and thereby takes recollection (as the condition of history) into the most interior, the most subjectivistic opposition to 'alienation' ['*Entäusserung*'] (as the condition of nature). Naturally, this inward, self-returning, subjectivistic sense of the word recollection would not have been usable if the concept [*Begriff*] had not been the guiding factor in the matter; but a reciprocal action of the inventions nonetheless exists."[21] In the hyphenation of *Er-Innerung* we suddenly see how speculation is dialectical. Its "seeing" (*specio*, to look at, behold) is dialectical. In the speculative act the mind's eye sees the thing in terms of the thing's own reality. The mind apprehends it not simply reflectively, in terms of its own knowing of it, but it beholds the thing known on the thing's own terms.

Cassirer, in a lecture on the philosophy of culture, quotes Hegel's views of *Erinnerung* at the end of the *Phenomenology* and emphasizes the difference between history as an activity of memory and that "arrived at in speculative metaphysical knowledge." Cassirer says, "For the historian, time is the true and in a certain sense the only dimension of his thought; it is the element in which history lives and moves and has its being. History must, therefore, always regard truth as an offspring of time: *Veritas filia Temporis*. But speculative philosophy cannot accept this view. Even when concerned with the phenomena of time, with the flux and reflux of history it is not satisfied within this sphere. It tends to rise above itself, to consider the realm of reality *sub quadam aeternitatis specio*."[22] Absolute knowing is speculative philosophy or metaphysics as dialectically conceived. The True is the whole, not in the sense that at the stage of the absolute all of experience is brought together as one, but in the sense that absolute knowing is a manner of seeing with the mind's eye *sub quadam aeternitatis*. Absolute knowing fits the classic definition of human wisdom as the ability to see things as they truly are.

Prudence is possible only when it can be derived from this contemplative standpoint of thought or *theoria*. To command absolute knowing is to hold in memory each stage of the experience of consciousness and to remember that each stage is not absolute. Each particular stage of consciousness believes it has conquered the phenomenon of "andness" that keeps the two moments of the opposition distinctive to that stage apart and that it has converted their andness into a unifying relation. Consciousness, caught up in the throes of each stage of its experience, suffers under this illusion of the achievement of synthesis or unity of its inherent oppositions.

To have absolute knowing is to see with total clarity that this believed unity is not so. To be wise is not to have this illusion in regard to each stage

---

21. Bloch, "Zerstörte-Sprache—zerstörte Kultur," 353–54. My translation. This was originally delivered by Bloch as a lecture in New York in 1939.

22. Cassirer, *Symbol, Myth, and Culture*, 80.

of consciousness. Thus the possession of the absolute form of knowing or consciousness achieved by the contemplation of all the forms of consciousness is to be able to move about in the world without illusion, knowing with complete confidence the limitations of each form. This is the meaning of Hegel's famous expression that the Owl of Minerva takes its flight only at the falling of the dusk.

Once the forms of experience have become the subject of contemplation, we possess the wisdom to move about in the world with prudence. The *Phenomenology*, and Hegel's corpus generally, is above all a book of instruction to the philosopher as to how to live and survive in the city. It is the *Ethik* of which he speaks in the "System-Program." The reader of the *Phenomenology* tends to regard its progress of forms as one being constructed forward from the previous one. But once the reader encounters Hegel's principle of the "we" (*wir*) as the observer of this progression, it is clear that the reader has traveled this "highway of despair" unaware before, but now, having in hand the text, can witness it, can recollect it *déjà vu*. It is a theater of memory, a vision of self-knowledge reached by recollection, not by any act of reflection. The reader acquires the wisdom of Mnemosyne.

Finally, this wisdom of absolute knowing is sublime. Hegel expresses this sublimity in his *Lectures on Fine Art*. He says, "The sublime in general is the attempt to express the infinite, without finding in the sphere of phenomena an object which proves adequate for this representation."[23] Art, along with religion, is the route spirit (*Geist*) takes to reach the philosophical or metaphysical sublime, the sublimity of the whole. Hegel says, "If therefore symbolic art in general may already be called sacred art because it adopts the Divine as the content of its productions, the art of sublimity is *the* sacred art as such which can be called exclusively sacred because it gives honour to God alone."[24] When the sublime enters art, art carries the meaning of Being as the proper object of religion. The experience of the sublime shows human beings their finitude and at the same time the infinitude of God. Hegel says, "So far as man is concerned, there are bound up with sublimity at the same time the sense of man's finitude and the insurmountable aloofness of God."[25]

23. Hegel, *Aesthetics*, 1:363.

24. Ibid., 1:372–73.

25. Ibid., 1:376. In his discussion of "Die Religion der Erhabenheit," in *Philosophie der Religion*, 50–96, Hegel associates this form of religion with ancient Judaism, as he also does in his treatment of the sublime in art.

From the religious sense of the sublime comes the metaphysical sublime, the grasp of the true infinity. The metaphysical absolute is the objective ground of the experience of the sublime. There can be no essential representation of the sublime. That is why the stages of the *Phenomenology* are a "gallery of images," but there is no *Bild* of the "*Begriff* of the *Begriff*" which is the sublime. The experience of the sublime is noetic, beyond the religious form of thought or *Vorstellen*.

The wisdom of absolute knowing is motivated by wonder, which is the antecedent to the sublime. Hegel writes, "Only spirit [*Geist*] is aware of spirit, wonder is only the presentiment of spirit, wonder is the interruption of nature; spirit is above all the true wonder over and against the course of nature. Spirit itself is only this awareness of itself."[26] Absolute knowing is *Geist* aware of itself by its ability to recollect all of itself in its totality of forms. Metaphysics is the ultimate form of thinking that acts against forgetting.

26. Hegel, "Die Religion der Erhabenheit," 93. My translation.

6

The Metaphysics of Symbolic Forms

Substance and Function

ERNST CASSIRER (1874–1945) BEGAN his career as part of the Marburg School of Neo-Kantianism, the central figures of which were Hermann Cohen and Paul Natorp. Some intellectual historians and writers of brief accounts of Cassirer's philosophy have mistakenly identified his philosophy of symbolic forms with this Neo-Kantian movement. While he never rejected the influence of his teacher, Hermann Cohen, Cassirer never regarded his philosophy of culture as simply an extension of Neo-Kantianism. When questioned by Heidegger about Neo-Kantianism, in their famous debate in Davos, Switzerland, in 1929, Cassirer responded that Neo-Kantianism must be understood in functional, rather than substantive, terms. Neo-Kantian philosophy should not be regarded as a single thing, a system of doctrine to which those associated with it must subscribe.[1]

Anyone who reads through the four volumes of the *Philosophy of Symbolic Forms* and the four volumes of *Das Erkennntnisproblem* will see, beyond a doubt, that among the many figures Cassirer discusses and cites, the two great sources for his system are Kant and Hegel. In his phenomenology of knowledge of the third volume of the *Philosophy of Symbolic Forms*, Cassirer says, "In speaking of a phenomenology of knowledge I am using the word 'phenomenology' not in its modern sense but with its fundamental signification as established and systematically grounded by Hegel" (PSF 3 xiv; viii). He follows this with an endorsement of Hegel's principle of the

---

1. See the translation of the Davos debate in Gordon, *Continental Divide*, chap. 4.

whole, which he states as *"Die Wahrheit is das 'Ganze,'"* an assertion he repeats in his metaphysics of his fourth volume. Having brought the problem of knowledge to its summation in Kant in the first two volumes of the *Erkenntnisproblem*, Cassirer proceeded to develop it on, to Hegel and beyond, in the following two volumes.

Cassirer understood that idealism develops from Kant to Hegel, and what is important is not the shoring up of the correctness of either Kant's or Hegel's philosophy but the philosophy of idealism itself. Without this approach, Cassirer's philosophy of symbol, myth, and culture would not have been possible. The critique of reason becomes the critique of culture, as Cassirer says, and then this critique becomes the basis for a total phenomenology of the functions of consciousness that underlie the forms of human knowledge and culture.

Cassirer's idealism can be regarded as the union of Kantian critique and Hegelian phenomenology. Each symbolic form—for example, science, language, and myth—can be analyzed in terms of the forms of intuition, of space, time, and number and the categories of object, causality, etc. There is a scientific intuition of space, a linguistic, a mythic, etc., and there is a scientific category of cause, a linguistic, a mythic, etc. The Kantian forms of intuition and categories are the internal structure of each symbolic form, although each invests them with a distinctive "tonality" (PSF 2:61; 75). They are each a type of knowledge that corresponds to a form of human culture.

Underlying this static source of symbolic forms is the dynamic sense, that they are interrelated as stages of development, each stage embodying a distinctive function of consciousness. The form of mythical thought is the product of the expressive function (*Ausdrucksfunktion*), the form of language of the representational function (*Darstellungsfunktion*), and the form of science of the significative (*Bedeutungsfunktion*) of consciousness.

In addition to these three forms that are the backbone of human knowledge and culture, Cassirer frequently speaks of a triad of myth, religion, and art. Religion is treated by Cassirer not as a separate symbolic form but as a development of mythical thought. In religion the mythic image is preserved but given an additional representational or scriptural meaning. Art, however, is a separate symbolic form. The aesthetic image is always an explicit or implicit recollection of the mythic image, yet the aesthetic image depends upon its own particular structuring of space, time, cause, etc.[2] Art is treated, as is history, as a symbolic form in Cassirer's summary

2. See Cassirer's comments on the reason he postponed, and never fully wrote, a

of the philosophy of symbolic forms in *An Essay on Man*. In it Cassirer also designates "myth and religion" as a single symbolic form.

In addition to these, Cassirer mentions as symbolic forms several forms of social life: economics (*die Wirtschaft*), technology (*die Technik*), ethics or morality (*die Sitte*), and law (*das Recht*) (PSF 2:xv; xi). Politics might be added to these as a potential symbolic form, on the basis of Cassirer's discussion in *The Myth of the State*, and regarding technology there is his early essay on "Form und Technik,"[3] but regarding economics, ethics, and law Cassirer does not provide even a tentative discussion. The symbolic forms of art and history arise in the development of consciousness as counterparts to natural science; they have their own manner of forming concepts, as Cassirer describes in *The Logic of the Cultural Sciences*. The student of Cassirer's system, however, is left to project how the symbolic forms of social life were specifically to be understood, should Cassirer have lived to complete his philosophy of symbolic forms.[4]

The key to all of Cassirer's philosophy, from his conception of the symbol to his conception of culture to his conception of metaphysics, is the replacement of substance with function. His systematic philosophy begins with his analysis of the opposition between substance-concepts and function-concepts, in the first chapter of his first statement of his theory of knowledge in *Substance and Function* (*Substanzbegriff und Funktionsbegriff* [1910]). Cassirer realized that the substance-based class of concepts of traditional Aristotelian logic had no relevance for the way in which concepts were actually formed in the natural sciences, but the senses of form evolving in modern or mathematical logic were relevant. What was needed was to put this issue in terms of a theory of knowledge.

The traditional theory of the generic concept (*Gattungsbegriff*) was an expression of Aristotelian metaphysics. The generic concept appears to be a natural form of thought. Nothing is presupposed except the existence of things in an inexhaustible multiplicity. To form the generic concept one needs only to fix in mind the properties that are common to several of them. These properties allow us to form a definition *per genus et differentia*. The mind proceeds by abstraction from *infima species* of sensuous particulars to ever-higher forms of classification by abandoning properties

---

volume on art, because of the *Ungunst* of the times, in *Symbol, Myth, and Culture*, 25.

3. For a translation of this essay see Cassirer, *The Warburg Years*.

4. For a full account of Cassirer's philosophy, see Verene, *Origins of the Philosophy of Symbolic Forms*.

until arriving at the most general category of all: "something," which can be affirmed of anything and everything.

Once thought has arrived at this ultimate point, however, the power of the concept to determine the particular has been entirely lost. This hierarchy of classification requires the support of substance metaphysics. As a logical process, the properties selected to designate a class of particulars supplies only what is called a "conventional definition." We must assume that any such definition has within it an "essential definition," that is, a statement of the essential property that distinguishes what is common only to these particulars and is simply accidental to others. The existence of such an essential property can be guaranteed only by a metaphysics of a hierarchy of substances to which such classes correspond. The order of thought requires this order of being. This requirement accounts for the fact that Aristotelian science can be only descriptive and can never achieve the hallmark of modern mathematically based or Galilean science, which is predictive.[5]

Aristotelian science is based on the subject-predicate structure of language. Modern science follows a logic of the quantitative function. For traditional class logic there exists the insoluble problem of quiddity or haecceity or thisness: what makes something be of a particular nature; what makes something be the type of thing that it is. How does the essential property that makes any particular be a member of a class such that it is both a member of the class and at the same time a true particular, differing from every other member of the class? The universal must enter into the being of each particular differently or each particular so enter into the universal. Otherwise the class has no members, or only a single member, which is identical with the class itself. If there is no way to discern one member's identity from another, the class is nothing more than an instance of the identity of indiscernibles. The solution must lie in claiming that each particular participates in the universal of the class in some progressive or proportionate way.

At this point we are at the threshold in which the substance-concept of class-membership, based on the subject-predicate structure of language, must give way to the function-concept of a serial whole. Cassirer puts it this way: the function-concept "is a new expression of the characteristic contrast between the *member of the series* and the *form of the series*. The

---

5. See Cassirer's informative essay "Influence of Language upon the Development of Scientific Thought," 309–27.

content of the concept cannot be dissolved into the elements of its extension, because the two do not lie on the same plane but belong in principle to
different dimensions. The meaning of the *law* that connects the individual
members is not to be exhausted by the enumeration of any number of instances of the law, for such enumeration lacks the generating *principle* that
enables us to connect the individual members into a functional whole."

The law of the series is of a different logical type than the members of
the series it orders. Thus the law of the series stands in the place of the generic concept or universal, and the members of the series stand in the place
of the particulars it claims to collect under a common essential property.
The difference is that the particular members form a series and the place
of each in it is determined by its relation to the law of the series. In the
function-concept, relation is essential. In the substance-concept, relations
between things are accidental to their identities.

Cassirer continues: "If I know the relation according to which *a*, *b*,
c . . . are ordered, I can deduce them by reflection and isolate them as objects of thought; it is impossible, on the other hand, to discover the special
character of the connecting relation from the mere juxtaposition of *a*, *b*, *c*
in presentation." It is not possible to regard the principle or law of the series
as an independent reality or substance, a thing, in contrast to the variables
of the series. Neither is it possible to regard these variables as independent
substances or things, for they have no identity or meaning apart from their
placement in the series in accordance with its law. Thus, "The serial form
$F(a, b, c \ldots)$ which connects the members of a manifold obviously cannot
be thought after the fashion of an individual a or b or c, without thereby
losing its peculiar character."[6] The function-concept has completely super-
seded the substance-concept.

The function-concept offers us a version of Hegel's "true infinite," as
discussed in the preceding chapter. Cassirer says, "Modern expositions of
logic have attempted to take account of this circumstance by opposing,—in
accordance with a well-known distinction of Hegel's,—the abstract universality of the concept to the concrete universality [*die konkrete Allgemeinheit*]
of the mathematical formula."[7] Hegel's *Begriff*, understood as the "concrete
concept," over and against the abstract concept of substance metaphysics,
has an internal, dialectical structure of particular and universal. The logical

6. Cassirer, *Substance and Function*, 26.

7. Ibid., 20. See Hegel's comments on the "mathematical infinite" vs. the "philosophical infinite" (SL 210–12; 247–49).

mechanism of this internal dialectic is expressed in the formula of the function-concept.

When Cassirer takes up the function-concept, in the third volume of the *Philosophy of Symbolic Forms*, he uses the notation of modern quantification theory, of $\varphi(\chi)$ (PSF 3:301; 346). Once we see that $\varphi(\chi)$ is a representation of the internal relation of the Hegelian *Begriff*, its inner form, we can immediately see that the logic of the true infinite is fully present in the *Begriff* itself. The (χ), taken alone as representing any series of χ_1, χ_2, χ_3, proceeds, in principle, infinitely, and thus is Hegel's bad infinite. Since it is a series, not a random, meaningless progression but a determinate order, continually formed by the principle φ, it is the representative of a true infinite. Moreover, if we consider φ as a possible variable, or (χ) in a higher series with the form $\varphi(\chi)$, and in a similar sense consider any member of this original series of (χ) as a φ principle of a subseries, the original conceptual structure of $\varphi(\chi)$ expands determinately and infinitely in all directions, at every point, the interconnection between φ and (χ) always being a whole.[8] This inner form becomes the mathematics, so to speak, of Hegel's dialectic of consciousness and thought.

Cassirer rejects the idea of a dialectic in which each content of consciousness seamlessly recapitulates itself and passes forward into a new form. He holds that in the development of human culture, forms and stages of its development often sharply confront each other. In fact, each symbolic form has within it a drive to dominate culture itself and subordinate all other forms to itself. The view of *aufheben*, discussed in the previous chapter, places Hegel's dialectic in accord with Cassirer's sense of dialectic as confrontation. When we recollect Hegel's stages of consciousness we should be astonished, not that they sometimes pass smoothly into their successors, but that there are any such seamless transitions at all. For often one stage simply confronts another, but consciousness manages to go on, because in fact we are simply recollecting the course it has already taken.

Symbolic Form

"Symbolic form" (*symbolische Form*) is the single term uniquely associated with Cassirer's philosophy. Implicit in it is Cassirer's conception of

---

8. It is likely that Cassirer believed that the concept of function can be connected to the concept of group, which occupied him later in his career; see "Concept of Group," 1–35, and his reflections on this issue in *Symbol, Myth, and Culture*, 271–91.

idealism. Cassirer begins the *Philosophy of Symbolic Forms* with this sentence: "Philosophical speculation began with the concept of *being*." And he continues: "In the very moment when this concept appeared, when man's consciousness awakened to the unity of being as opposed to the multiplicity and diversity of existing things, the specific philosophical approach to the world was born" (PSF 1:73; 1). Philosophical idealism, for Cassirer, begins with Plato's discovery of *eidos* (of form, the idea). Cassirer says, of Plato's theory of ideas, "The great systematic and historical achievement of this theory of ideas is that here, for the first time, the essential intellectual premise for any philosophical understanding and explanation of the world took on explicit form" (PSF 1:73; 1–2).

The origins of philosophy and idealism are one. Without the idea there is no philosophy. As Whitehead says, in one of his most famous remarks, "The sagest general characterization of the European philosophical tradition is that it consists of a series of footnotes to Plato" (PR 63). By this assertion, Whitehead does not mean the specific scheme of Platonic thought that can be extracted from Plato's writings but rather "the wealth of general ideas scattered through them."

The philosophy of the idea has always faced the problem of whether ideas are copies of things or whether things are themselves ideas. Cassirer says, "It is not the case, however, that the symbolic signs which we encounter in language, myth, and art first 'are' and then, beyond this 'being,' achieve a certain meaning; their being arises from their signification." He says, "Myth and art, language and science, are in this sense configurations *towards* being: they are not simple copies of an existing reality but represent the main directions of the spiritual movement, of the ideal process by which reality is constituted for us as one and many—as a diversity of forms which are ultimately held together by a unity of meaning" (PSF 1:106–7; 40–41).

Cassirer points out that, should we wish to believe that ideas in the sense of symbols were nothing but a repetition of an already fixed content, we would be faced with two questions. What would be accomplished by having a copy of something that is already present for the mind? And further, how could an exact copy ever be accomplished? A copy of anything is never perfectly equal to the original, or it would simply be the original. We know only through ideas, the medium of which are the symbols of the activity of mind or *Geist*. Thus what we know must be that which can be constructed through the idea. What is for us is always a product of what we can know it to be.

The direct source for Cassirer's conception of the symbol is Kant's conception of the schematism. Having distinguished concepts or categories from appearances or sensuous intuitions, Kant, in the *Critique of Pure Reason*, reaches the point at which the question arises of how the two are to be related. Kant says, "Obviously there must be some third thing, which is homogeneous on the one hand with the category, and on the other hand with the appearance, and which thus makes the application of the former to the latter possible. This mediating representation must be pure, that is, void of all empirical content, and yet at the same time, while it must in one respect be *intellectual*, it must in another be *sensible*. Such a representation is the *transcendental schema*."[9]

In his doctrine of the schema, Kant has reached, in terms of a theory of the knowing subject, the same problem Plato faced in metaphysical terms: how the particular existent participates in a form. Both Plato and Kant face the difficulty of the so-called "third man argument," namely, if the form is to be related to the particular instance of it, or the concept to the intuition in terms of a "third thing," the issue arises as to how, on the one hand, this third thing is related to the form or concept, and on the other hand how it is related to the particular or sensuous intuition. The third man argument thus sets up an indefinite regress of relations that cannot be summed, for to sum an indefinite regress is a contradiction.

Kant's "solution" to this problem is to declare that "this schematism of our understanding, in its application to appearances and their mere form, is an art concealed in the depths of the human soul [*ist eine verborgene Kunst in den Tiefen der menschlichen Seele*], whose real modes of activity nature is hardly likely ever to allow us to discover, and to have open to our gaze."[10] It is clear that the opposition of our concepts and our sensuous intuitions are joined in the mind's act of knowing, because we possess intellectually formed empirical knowledge, but Kant is unable to say how this truly is possible. It is like Zeno's paradoxes; the runner obviously reaches the end of the stadium and the hare obviously overtakes the tortoise, but we lack a rational account to justify it. The joining of thought with sensibility is the very principle of human experience, but Kant is unable to produce a phenomenon in experience that makes experience in the sense of the schema possible. Kant's analysis of experience can show only that such a schema is necessary.

9. Kant, *Critique of Pure Reason*, 181.
10. Ibid., 183.

Kant says that "the schema is in itself always a product of imagination [*Einbildungskraft*]." He says further that the schema is to be distinguished from the image (*Bild*). Kant is incorporating into his epistemology the longstanding view that the imagination is a middle term between the intellect and the senses. The image forms what is sensed and readies it to be reformed as a thought. Kant says, "This representation of a universal procedure of imagination in providing an image for a concept, I entitle the schema of this concept."[11] The role of the imagination as Kant states it here is largely passive. It brings together the diversity of immediate sensations but its activity is limited to this assemblage. The object is made in thought in its conception. Kant also has an active sense of the imagination insofar as the schema of a pure concept is a transcendental product of imagination. The active power of the imagination has a resonance with Cassirer's conception of the symbol as connected to the inner form of culture.

Cassirer solves the problem of the art lost in the human soul with his theory of the symbol. If Kant's location in the process of knowledge is correct that a "third thing" is required, it must be possible to locate it in experience. Cassirer finds this in the phenomenon of the symbol that unites both an active and a passive sense of the imagination. His full statement of this sense of the symbol is centered in the term "symbolic 'pregnance'" (*symbolische Prägnanz*), a term that has origins in the "law of pregnance" of Gestalt psychology and connections to Leibniz's *praegnans futuri*, as any symbolic act, as Cassirer says, is saturated with the future. Any given symbol is always an element in a system of symbols. Cassirer says, "By symbolic pregnance we mean the way in which a perception as a sensory experience contains at the same time a certain nonintuitive meaning which it immediately and concretely represents. Here we are not dealing with bare perceptive data, on which some sort of apperceptive acts are later grafted, through which they are interpreted, judged, transformed" (PSF 3: 202; 231).

A symbol is at once something physical and something mental (*geistig*). A spoken word is a breath of air, yet it carries a meaning. A written word is a mark on a surface, yet it also carries a meaning. The twofold factors of this single entity are as inseparable as those of the functional $\varphi\ (\chi)$. Cassirer does not regard Husserl's phenomenology as having overcome this problem of *Sinn im Sinnlichkeit*, of the sense in the sensible. He says, "Husserl dissects the whole of experience into two halves; primary contents, which still contain no meaning, and experiences or factors of experience,

11. Ibid., 182.

which are grounded in a specific intentionality" (PSF 3:198; 226–27). Cassirer claims that while Husserl's "hyletic" and "noetic" factors are never separable in any absolute sense in consciousness, they are "to a great extent independent variables in respect to each other" (PSF 3:199–200; 228). Husserl has not overcome Kant's problem of the two orders of experience through his method of descriptive phenomenology. Husserl has cast it in terms of phenomena, but has not overcome the inherent diremption between the sensible and the spiritual, of material and its form. We are still left with the two strata of consciousness.

Cassirer verifies his conception of symbolic pregnance with a single thought-experiment. He asks his reader to consider a graph-like line drawing (*Linienzug*). We may first, he says, apprehend it as having a distinct physiognomic character, as expressing a particular mood. The line has an up and down dynamic; it may also be rounded, or break off and be jagged. It may appear hard or soft. The line is there, but what is there depends immediately upon how we feel it and absorb it into our consciousness. We may pass from this expressive immediate grasp of the nature of the line to holding the line at a mental distance, regarding it as a mathematical structure, a geometric figure. All the individual properties of the line are absolutely irrelevant to this second apprehension of it. Any sense of the rhythm or mood it embodies is put aside. It represents a trigonometric function. Its total meaning is exhausted in its presentation of its analytical formula. It is only a paradigm for this formula. To understand the figure in this way is also to have it linked with the totality of geometric forms.

We can pass from the line as a geometric object to apprehending it as a mythical symbol dividing sacred from profane space. The line then has mythical or magical power to warn us of the profane and attract us to the sacred precinct. We can turn from the line as having this mythic significance and see it as an aesthetic ornament. There is no such thing as the line in itself, apart from our symbolic grasp of it. Each of these contexts structures the line as a particular of each form through which it is apprehended.

Cassirer gives a second thought-experiment in a late lecture on the philosophy of history. He says, "Let me assume that in a shipwreck I am, like Robinson Crusoe, driven to a desert island. I am perfectly abandoned; I can detect no traces of human life or human culture. When walking on the shore I find by chance a stone which by its unusual size or form attracts my attention." Cassirer says I may first regard the stone in empirical, scientific terms, taking up the perspective of a mineralogist or geologist.

But then, he says, imagine that I discover that the stone has a number of marks on it, and suddenly I think these marks may be more than physical indentations in the stone. They may be part of a system of written characters, part of a language. He says, "I am introduced by them not only into a physical world, but also into a human world—not into a mere world of things, but into a world of symbols." Now, Cassirer says, I am in the position of a historian having discovered an artifact that must not only be understood in general human terms, it must be interpreted in terms of its connection to the symbolic form of history, which combines both the symbolic forms of empirical science and of art in regard to the narration of the significance of the artifact. Cassirer says, "This intellectual and imaginative synthesis is what we call history—just as much as the synthesis of particular material phenomena in space and time according to general laws is called natural science."[12]

Cassirer states his most succinct definition of a symbolic form as: "By 'symbolic form,' one should understand every energy of spirit by which the content of spiritual signification is linked to a concrete and intrinsically appropriate sensuous sign."[13] As Kant connects the imagination to the schema, so does Cassirer. But Cassirer's theory requires that a different sense of the imagination is necessary to the symbol than was necessary to the schema. The passive role of the empirical imagination must be joined to a fully active sense of the imagination in its power of inventiveness—the power to make or form the perceived object, not merely to transmit the sensed object in the form of the image to the intellect's production of conceptual structures or to produce these structures in their pure form. The sense of imagination required is similar to Vico's *fantasia*, as the "making imagination." Cassirer, without discussing symbolic form explicitly in these terms, requires this fully concrete sense of the imagination. Rather than the imagination attaching itself to reason, reason is led by the imagination. This connection is no more evident than in both Vico's and Cassirer's conception of mythical thought as the original form of consciousness.

The symbolic form of myth produces a total order of the world through the power of the imagination to symbolize. There is no literal or rational interpretation of the world that consciousness first forms and then proceeds to narrate in primal and societal, mythic images. The world is

---

12. Cassirer, *Symbol, Myth, and Culture*, 135–37.

13. Cassirer, "The Concept of Symbolic Form in the Construction of the Human Sciences," in *Warburg Years*, 76.

first felt as an opposition of benign and malignant forces that are made into images by the active power of the imagination. These feelings of the benign and the malignant generate the opposition between the sacred and the profane, the opposition through which consciousness first experiences the world. All of Cassirer's philosophy of culture is founded on the primacy of mythical thought. To put this point in Hegelian terms, Cassirer discovers the sense in which myth, as a symbolic form, is the teacher of humanity.

Spirit and Life

For Cassirer, philosophy has a normative role in human culture. In his inaugural lecture, on his appointment to the University of Göteborg, Sweden, in 1935, "The Concept of Philosophy as a Philosophical Problem," Cassirer distinguishes two concepts of philosophy. One he calls the "scholastic" concept of philosophy; the other is a concept of philosophy as "related to the world." These are two duties of philosophy, and the second proceeds from the first. Philosophy must be concerned with the perfection of knowledge and with the systematic unity of all the forms of knowing. But it must bring this perspective and acumen to bear on human events.

If we comprehend this distinction well, we will see that moral philosophy cannot be pursued *sui generis* apart from metaphysics. In like manner, metaphysics cannot be a form of thought that bears no results for the ancient pursuits of self-knowledge and citizenship. Real philosophy requires the joint pursuit of both metaphysics and moral philosophy. One cannot substitute for the other. The real and the moral are twins. We find them joined in the figure of Socrates. The question, for the modern philosopher, is how this double obligation of philosophy can be continued. Too easily, in the modern world, as discussed earlier, philosophy dissolves into politics, with its tendencies to ideology and relativism of truth.

Cassirer says, "Without the claim to an independent, objective, and autonomous truth, not only philosophy, but also each particular field of knowledge, natural science as well as the humanities, would lose their stability and their sense."[14] In regard to the normative role of philosophy, Cassirer cites Albert Schweitzer, whom, he says, has raised the basic question of the duty of philosophy in the present time. Cassirer is speaking in exile, in a world facing the rise of Nazism. Schweitzer claims that it is not, nor can it be, the task of philosophy to bring moral order into the world. Philosophy

14. Cassirer, *Symbol, Myth, and Culture*, 61.

is the ultimate guide and caretaker of reason in general. Its duty is to be this caretaker, and speak on behalf of reason; to direct the attention of the educated and the uneducated to the problem of cultural ideals. Schweitzer says, "But in the hour of peril the watchman slept, who should have kept watch over us. So it happened that we did not struggle for our culture."[15]

Philosophy is the repository of reason when events go against the human. It is, in the end, the only place to which we may turn. In order to act or even to preserve ourselves, we must understand events fully and precisely. Philosophy, then, is the watchman, the conscience, that culture continually requires, and without which there is no culture. There is merely politics.

Cassirer takes the twofold distinction of the nature of philosophy from Kant's "The Architectonic of Pure Reason." He says philosophy must not accept the satisfaction in the power of reason that was characteristic of the eighteenth-century Enlightenment thinkers, and he says philosophy also cannot accept the nineteenth-century Hegelian assertion that "what is rational is real; and what is real is rational." If this claim, Cassirer holds, is taken to mean that reason is an immanent, substantive, eternal presence in things, we must put it aside. He says we must not think that reason is a constant presence in affairs. Reason is not a given; it is a task. Cassirer says that "we must seek it [reason] in the continual self-renewing work of spirit."[16] Reason, for Cassirer, is the self-determining aspect of thought, and in this sense it is the agent of human freedom. This sense of reason goes between the pragmatic employment of reason as an instrument of action and growth and the purely theoretical conception of reason as independent from human affairs.

Cassirer concludes *An Essay on Man* with the statement: "Human culture taken as a whole may be described as the process of man's progressive self-liberation. Language, art, religion, science are various phases in this process."[17] Each symbolic form competes with the others for its place in culture. But Cassirer says they cannot be reduced to a common denominator. He says, "All these functions complete and complement one another. Each one opens a new horizon and shows us a new aspect of humanity. The dissonant is in harmony with itself; the contraries are not mutually exclusive, but interdependent: 'harmony is contrariety, as in the case of the

15. Ibid., 60. Quoted by Cassirer from Schweitzer's Olaus-Petri lectures, delivered at the University of Uppsala in 1922.

16. Ibid. 62.

17. Cassirer, *Essay on Man*, 228.

bow and the lyre.'"[18] Culture is a dialectically ordered whole: "For this is a dialectic unity, a coexistence of contraries."[19] The duty of philosophy is to project this ideal of cultural harmony to the times.

Philosophy is not a symbolic form. Cassirer is quite definite on this point. He says, "It is characteristic of philosophical knowledge as the 'self-knowledge of reason' that it does not create a principally new symbol form, it does not found in this sense a new creative modality—but it grasps the earlier modalities as that which they are: as characteristic symbolic forms." Philosophy is essentially self-knowledge. In the harmony in contrariety of the symbolic forms taken as a whole, the human self sees itself. It is what it makes. This wisdom is what philosophy teaches. Cassirer says further, "Philosophy does not want to replace the older forms with another, higher form. It does not want to replace one symbol with another; rather, its task consists in comprehending the basic symbolic character of knowledge itself" (PSF 4:226; 264–65).

This conception of the relation of philosophy to the array of symbolic forms in each of their modalities is functional. Philosophy stands to the particular symbolic forms as φ stands to (χ). Philosophy is the law, so to speak, of their serial arrangement. Like the series of variables χ_1, χ_2, χ_3, no form of culture has a meaning in and of itself, apart from its interconnections with culture as a whole. In like manner, philosophy is a form of thinking without content if it is not an activity in culture itself, if it is not culture comprehended in its most complete terms. There is no Absolute that stands as a substance beyond the individual symbolic forms, to which each teleologically advances. Cassirer says, "The 'Absolute' is always simply the completely relative, which has been carried through to the end in a systematic overview, and the absoluteness of geist in particular can be nothing else and cannot try to be" (PSF 4:227; 265).

The view of Hegel developed in the preceding chapter herein would not disagree with this conception of the Absolute as internal to every stage of the development of consciousness. Cassirer intends to replace the "block universe" interpretation of the traditional conception of a system of philosophical idealism with the principle of "systematic review." The terms Cassirer substitutes for system are "systematic overview" (*systematischer Überblick*), "systematic review" (*systematischer Rückblick*), or "systematic reconstruction" (*systematischer Rekonstruktion*) (e.g., see PSF 4:56; 54). By

18. Ibid. Cassirer's reference is to Heraclitus (fr. 51).
19. Ibid., 222.

"systematic," Cassirer means that as the law of a series φ determines systematically the position of each variable χ in a series, philosophy determines the position of each symbolic form in the totality of human culture. Culture without philosophy as its principle of harmony is a fragmented collection of human activity, having no rational knowledge of itself.

Cassirer's view of philosophy as systematic overview is taken from the Enlightenment. In his *Philosophy of the Enlightenment*, Cassirer says, "But in renouncing and even in directly opposing the 'spirit of systems' (*esprit de système*), the philosophy of the Enlightenment by no means gives up the 'systematic spirit' (*esprit systématique*)." The systematic spirit takes philosophy directly into the inner form of each of the fields of knowledge. Cassirer concludes, "Philosophy, according to this interpretation, is no special field of knowledge situated beside or above the principles of natural science, of law and government, etc., but rather the all-comprehensive medium in which principles are formulated, developed, and founded."[20] Cassirer says, "Were it not for this previous synthesis effected by the sciences themselves philosophy would have no starting point."[21]

Philosophy is systematic review, and at the same time it is recollective memory. The watchman remembers and can call us back, at crucial moments in history, to the moments when there was cultural harmony in the natural oppositions of culture and knowledge. Reason sets the standard, not in terms of reducing the multiplicity of symbolic forms and fields of knowledge to the single form of logic, but in terms of the possibilities of a concrete order of things. Barbarism and rational madness occur when that has been forgotten. It is recollection joined with reason that humanizes and preserves humanity.

Culture is the reality in which we find ourselves, but in what reality does culture find itself? This is the question Cassirer faces in his metaphysics of spirit (*Geist*) and life (*Leben*). Kantian philosophy can offer us no guidance in this question because, as the critique of reason is transformed into the critique of culture, producing the analyses of the structures of the various symbolic forms, the question of the thing-in-itself is not solved. Kant has put metaphysics aside. When this question of the nature of the real is posed, the philosopher, confined within the limits of transcendental idealism, must look the other way. To face the question of the real, Cassirer thus turns to the primary term of Hegelian idealism—*Geist*—and to the

20. Cassirer, *Philosophy of the Enlightenment*, vii.
21. Cassirer, *Essay on Man*, 71.

Hegelian method of opposites—dialectic. Cassirer assumes the opposition of spirit and life as it developed from metaphysics in the nineteenth and early twentieth centuries. He says, "The opposition between 'Leben' and 'Geist' is the hub of this metaphysics; it proves to be so definitive and decisive that it gradually comes to absorb into itself and eliminate all other pairs of metaphysical terms that have been coined in the history of metaphysics. The opposites of 'Being' and 'Becoming,' of 'One' and 'Many,' 'Matter' and 'Form,' 'Soul' and 'Body' all appear to have been dissolved into this one completely fundamental antithesis" (PSF 4:8; 7–8).

Cassirer, having grounded his thought in the internal dialectic of the function, knows that the solution to understanding the coincidence of these opposites cannot be solved by embracing one side of the opposition over the other. Spirit and life also are not to be understood as two separate substances that can only be united by a third thing. Spirit and life must be understood as a process in which life achieves what it inherently is through a transformative activity into spirit, and spirit is what it is, not as a being independent of life but as the ongoing transformation of the force of life into a self-ordering process. Cassirer is specifically responding to *Lebensphilosophie*, which he defines quite widely to include Scheler, Simmel, Heidegger, and Bergson. He also associates this position with Schopenhauer, Kierkegaard, and Nietzsche. Each of these figures, for Cassirer, to some extent sees the human being as alienated from the unique product of human activity—culture. They wish, in different ways, to bring the human back to the original unity of life. Cassirer, instead, conceives spirit as the counterpart of life, while acknowledging that life is also a necessary basis of culture.

Cassirer explains his conception of the functional relation of spirit and life as a solution to the problems he finds in Simmel's *Lebensphilosophie*. He says that, in Simmel's concept of life, "life's actual movement consists in the oscillation between two extreme phases. It is never at one with itself except by being beyond itself at the same time" (PSF 4:9; 9). The general claim that life is a unity is in fact simply a presupposition, because life demonstrates no principle of unity that governs it. Life does not maintain itself as a reality independent of spirit. Instead, spirit just as much makes life what it is as life makes spirit what it is.

Cassirer is not advancing a more adequate version of *Lebensphilosophie,* nor is he replacing it with a *Philosophie des Geistes*. Cassirer is a metaphysical dualist. But this is a functional dualism. The unity of the real lies in the simple fact that each side of the opposition of spirit and life requires the other to be and to be what it is. Spirit and life are a functional bond of self-formation, whose internal movement is dialectical. Cassirer says, "No matter how we regard it or proclaim it as the original source of all reality, life in itself is never the source of the symbols in which this reality is first comprehended and understood, in which it 'speaks to us'" (PSF 4:30; 29–30).

Life has only the power to flow on in its immediacy. It cannot recapitulate itself. Spirit, unlike life, has the power to turn about on itself, thus embodying the principle of self-knowing that is at the foundation of culture. Cassirer says, "This turnabout, this 'reflection,' entails no break with geist itself; rather, it is the form in which it proves itself and reconfirms itself, something that is characteristic of and typical of it alone. So what threatens constantly to tear it asunder is also what always brings it back to itself; this being two-in-one is its true fate and represents its actual achievement" (PSF 4:33; 32). The two-in-one that characterizes the coincidence of the opposition between spirit and life is taken up within the life of spirit. This ability to take up opposites is what gives spirit its distinctive mode of being. Spirit, in so doing, is freed from the immediacy that controls life.

Cassirer says, "The philosophy of symbolic forms has sought from the beginning to establish the path that leads through the concrete productions of geist. By taking this path, the philosophy of symbolic forms finds that it meets with geist everywhere as not the 'Will to Power,' but as the 'Will to Formation'" (PSF 4:28; 27). This fundamental power of spirit is the basis of human freedom as self-determination, in which the knower gains mental distance from the immediacy of the object known and also can transfer this process on to the selfhood of the knower. The self can make itself its own object.

The answer to *Lebensphilosophie* is not the affirmation of the positive being of spirit. It is the conception of a metaphysics that acknowledges both sides of the opposition of life and spirit as a functional dualism—spirit is the self-reflective rule by which the moments of the flow of life are formed as an ordered series of variables. Cassirer's metaphysical dualism is a restatement of the standpoint of Hegel's phenomenology, put forth as an answer to the problems raised by *Lebensphilosophie*. Cassirer claims, "The fundamental thesis of 'Objective Idealism' completely maintains its ground, in the face of all the criticism which the nineteenth and twentieth centuries' 'philosophy of life' has urged against it. Especially as concerns Hegel, it would be a complete misunderstanding of his system to bring against it the reproach that by reason of its panlogistic tendency it denies the rights of Life—that it has sacrificed the vital sphere to that of logic."[22]

We may finally ask, what is not achieved in Cassirer's metaphysics of spirit and life? Cassirer has not presented a doctrine of being, or of God. There is no Cassirerian cosmology, such as in A. N. Whitehead's *Process and Reality*. What Cassirer has offered is literally a metaphysics of symbolic forms. It is a broadly stated account of the fundamental opposition that lies at the basis of the human world of knowledge and culture. It thus provides the symbolic forms a context. It is a transcendental metaphysics. Spirit and life as universal forces are transcendent of the individual but they are not an opposition within a providential order. Cassirer's metaphysics of symbolic forms holds to Alexander Pope's line: "Know then thyself, presume not God to scan, / The proper study of mankind is man" (Epistle 2, line 1). This is the line upon which Cassirer bases *An Essay on Man*.

Basisphenomena

Spirit is a function of life attained through the symbol. The result is the human world, set off by its mentality from the non-human, animal world. Cassirer holds that animal mentality is capable of sign behavior but not of the responses produced in human mentality by the symbol. The sign has a one-to-one correspondence to the thing signified. The symbol is self-modifying. It re-presents the thing in its own medium, such that it can signify itself becoming part of a system of symbols. The symbol is dialectical in the way that human consciousness can apprehend its object and then apprehend its apprehension of the object. The human world is what humans make it to be, and in so doing the being of the human being is also made. Human being is a functional circle of mental and physical activity. There is not a fixed, substantive human nature to which certain properties adhere. The human being as *animal rationale* becomes *animal symbolicum*. To reason is to employ symbols.

In *An Essay on Man*, Cassirer transforms his metaphysical analysis of the interrelation of spirit and life into the analysis of the organism of the biology of Jakob von Uexküll. In Uexküll's biology, every organism occupies an *Umwelt*, an environment of its own into which it is fitted. In accord with its anatomical structure, it has a *Merknetz* (a receptor system) and a *Wirknetz* (an effector system). The organism must internally coordinate

22. Cassirer, "'Spirit' and 'Life' in Contemporary Philosophy," 875.

these two systems in order to survive. By means of the receptor system the organism receives stimuli externally, and through the effector system it re-acts to them. These two systems, then, are functions of each other. In higher animals the functioning of these two systems is the basis of sign behavior. A dog can react to the stimulus "rats" and look immediately to find them as prey. But the dog does not entertain the abstract idea of "rats" as a class concept, nor can the dog respond to this idea by considering it in relation to an entire system of language.

Cassirer says that the human animal's power of the symbolic act is a middle term between these two systems. He says, "Between the receptor system and the effector system, which are to be found in all animal species, we find in man a third link which we may describe as the *symbolic system*. This new acquisition transforms the whole of human life. As compared with the other animals man lives not merely in a broader reality; he lives, so to speak, in a new *dimension* of reality."[23] In biological terms it is this third system that allows for the transformation of life into spirit.

From this biological account of the distinctively human we can turn back to Cassirer's phenomenological account that supplements his meta-physical doctrine of spirit and life. If spirit is a transformation of life, and thus the basis of the human world, how does the human world actually constitute itself as the manifestation of spirit? Cassirer's answer is his theory of basisphenomena (*Basisphänomene*). To formulate this theory he turns to the poets, to Goethe. If Kant and Hegel are Cassirer's two great sources of his philosophy among his many sources, Goethe is the great poetic source that runs throughout his work. Cassirer finds in Goethe's maxims the meanings for the basisphenomena he seeks. Cassirer says, "Here our question arises: . . . How can we do justice to the Goethean demand for the recognition of 'primary phenomena' and to the Cartesian-Kantian demand for 'reflection' in knowledge and philosophy?" (PSF 4:136; 130). Goethe's poetic sense of the human that is expressed in his maxims 391–93 must be given a philosophical formulation. These maxims concern the nature of the self, the other, and the pursuit of self-realization.[24]

Cassirer characterizes the first of the basisphenomena as "the phe-nomenon of the '*I*,' of the *monas* of 'life' itself." He says that "this cannot be

---

23. Cassirer, *Essay on Man*, 24.

24. Goethe, *Maximen und Reflexionen*, 76–77. Cassirer, in his manuscript, quotes only the first lines of maxim 391, followed by ellipses. The texts of the three maxims are supplied in the English translation (see PSF 4:127–28). They can be found in the German edition in the editors' notes; see 336–37.

inferred from something else, but instead lies at the basis of everything else" (PSF 4:138; 133). Goethe's maxim 391 describes life as a rotating movement of the monad around itself. Goethe says, "The impulse to nurture this life is ineradicably implanted in each individual, although its specific nature remains a mystery to ourselves and to others" (PSF 4:127). Cassirer interprets this sense of the human monad as "a process, as movement—the 'stream of consciousness' which constantly flows and knows neither rest nor quiet" (PSF 4:128; 123). Life exists not as a general movement; its movement is in terms of centers or monads, similar to Leibnizian monads in that their movement is within themselves. There is also a "windowless" dimension to these monads because others do not have access to this movement of life within ourselves, and even we do not comprehend this internal ceaseless movement, our sense of being continually alive, which we nurture without knowing why in any reflective sense.

Cassirer says that this monadic being "is not bound to a particular moment, but rather encompasses the totality of all aspects of life, the present, past, and future" (PSF 4:139; 133–34). The I as monadic being is not a developed individual self with subjectivity set off against an external world. It *is* the world, and it is in constant flux. One state of its existence simply gives way to another, in a movement of immediacy. There is no memory at this primary level. The past, present, and future are one continuous process, each moment giving way to the next. There is no clear boundary between I and world or other. The monad is a center of activity; it is not a fixed thing with its own certain identity.

Goethe's maxim 392 concerns the living and moving monad's intervention in the world, a process in which it meets definite limits—limits that are not experienced in regard to its internal life. Goethe says of this intervention, "Through this it becomes truly aware of itself as internal lack of limits, and as externally limited. Although it requires a predisposition, attention, and luck, we can become clear ourselves about what we experience; but to others it remains a mystery" (PSF 4:127). Cassirer says this is a process of "becoming aware" in the sense of doing—both action and reaction. "The 'life' of the *monas* does not remain a kind of closed existence" (PSF 4:128; 123–24). He calls this process the basis phenomenon of "action" (*Wirken*). In this going out to the world, the monadic "I" transcends its "windowless," self-rotating movement and takes on the additional movement of a reaching out. This reaching out is an action. This action is at the basis of the I as a social process. Yet in this social process the other, toward which its action is directed, can have no real experience of the inner life of the acting monad. The monadic being experiences opposition in and through its action as something standing over and against its own life-process.

Cassirer says that "this 'standing in opposition,' this 'resistance' is originally encountered in the experience of the will, but not a merely impersonal 'It' [*Es*]. Rather, we find it originally as a 'Thou' [*Du*]" (PSF 4:140; 134–35). This relation to an other is not as such social in any developed sense of community. It is just the most fundamental sense of living together that the human shares with the animal world. It is analogous to what Whitehead calls a "nexus." But, Cassirer says, "we want to emphasize this one point, that this form of being-with-one-another in the form of having influence-on-one-another is a genuine Basis Phenomenon; it can be derived from nothing else, but is originally constitutive" (PSF 4:140; 135). This phenomenon is the presupposition of the claim that human beings are by nature social animals. It is from this phenomenon that human society develops.

Cassirer makes the same claim of non-derivability for this second basis phenomenon as he does for the first. Here we are also still at the level of life, except now life has expanded its movement from the inner rotation of the monad to the outer flow of the monad to the other. The other of the monad, however, is an other of itself. It is not a pure other, diverse in its form of being. But this sense of other as "Thou" provides the basis for the moral in human experience. At its basis the moral must derive from sympathy or empathy for that which is not I. *Synderesis* or the inborn knowledge of the principles of moral action and conscience originates here. Without this "*Wirkens-Phänomen*" there could be no morality developed to guide human affairs. Without the "*Ich-Phänomen*" there could be no will to self-preservation that tempers and directs all individual action and so preserves society.

Goethe's maxim 393 points to the fact that our actions toward the outer world do not remain ours or under our control. They require, and take on, as they develop into specifically human actions, forms of speech and writing. These come to belong to the outer world more than they belong to us. Our productions of imagination and thought often provide the other of the outer world to gain a better understanding of ourselves than we are able to obtain. Goethe says, "However, in the outer world one senses that in order to really be clear about this, it is necessary to learn as much as possible about what we have experienced. This is why people are so greatly interested in youthful beginnings, stages of education, biographical details, anecdotes, and the like" (PSF 4:127–28).

Our actions must be put in terms that are not simply of our own possession. This formation of our thoughts and actions in speech and writing is necessary for us to experience ourselves. In such we mirror and create ourselves, yet what we create does not and cannot remain ours. Cassirer says, "Others can know us only in our work, as what we do and make, as what we say and write, as *praxis* and *poiesis* (Aristotle)" (PSF 4:130; 125). Our works also outlive us as their creator. They possess a peculiar kind of transcendence. The "I" can sustain itself, its life, only by transposing its inner rotation into an outer, spiritual form. This third basis phenomenon is the basis of culture itself.

Cassirer calls the third basis phenomenon "the sphere of the work" (PSF 4:141; 136). The term in German is *Werk*, in the sense of the artwork or the literary work, the *oeuvre* as opposed to labor or *Arbeit*. The work is something that is made, a *factum*. The work opens up for us the sense of the objective world that can be represented in the work. Thus the work is not simply an expression of the subjective. Any expression of the subjective, to the extent that it claims to be more than simple utterance or outcry, is potentially a work or the basis for a work. The work allows us to be in the world on our own terms, not simply to be in it. The *Werk-Phänomen* is a primary human phenomenon. It is not derived from anything more basic than itself. These three phenomena are that from which we can derive all that is in the human world. Cassirer says, "Here we have the three primary phenomena (basis phenomena) before us, for which we ourselves cannot give any further 'explanation' and cannot want to" (PSF 4:142; 137). Cassirer regards these as the key to human reality and to human culture—"*die Schlüssel zur 'Wirklichkeit' sind*."

The monadic "I" and action toward the other are not as such especially original with Cassirer. Although Cassirer has his own version of them as reflections on the insights of Goethe's maxims, versions of them populate phenomenological literature. Particular to Cassirer is his eliciting of the phenomenon of the work, because it is so closely connected to his concept of culture as the product of the symbol. The work presupposes the other two basis phenomena. It could not function without them, but their meaning would be quite different without their culmination in the work. The symbol system that distinguishes the human animal necessarily implies the work. Philosophy becomes the ultimate act of the work in that its reflective and speculative grasp of the individual forms of culture shows us what culture is, and in so doing shows us what we ourselves are.

7

Process, Reality, and God

Ideas

THE PHILOSOPHY OF ALFRED North Whitehead (1861–1947) brings together a theory of science, speculative philosophy, and civilization based on
the set of great ideas pursued in Western society and thought from ancient
Greece and Rome to medieval and modern Europe.[1] Our understanding of
the world, reflected in our ordering experience, science, and metaphysics,
originates, in Whitehead's view, from ideas expressed by Plato. Whitehead
says, "His later dialogues circle round seven notions, namely—The
Ideas, The Physical Elements, The Psyche, The Eros, The Harmony, The
Mathematical Relations, The Receptacle. I mention them because I hold
that all philosophy is in fact an endeavor to obtain a coherent system out
of some modification of these notions" (AI 354). Whitehead says that Plato
left no system of metaphysics but he left these great ideas to be developed.
To develop them we must start from actuality being a physical process in
which the past transforms itself into a new creation, and in which the mind
or soul comes to entertain new ideas.

Civilization, Whitehead holds, is realized through the pursuit of truth,
beauty, art, adventure, and peace. These five qualities guide history, and
the human endeavors within it, toward civilization. In summing up his account of these in his *Adventures of Ideas*, Whitehead says, "The gradual

---

1. Whitehead says that his three books *Science and the Modern World*, *Process and
Reality*, and *Adventures of Ideas* are a trilogy that constitutes an endeavor to express a way
of understanding things. See AI vii.

emergence of such modes, and their effect on human history, have been among the themes of this book in its appeal to history. We have found the growth of Art: its gradual sublimation into the pursuit of Truth and Beauty: the sublimation of the egoistic aim by its inclusion of the transcendent whole: the youthful zest in the transcendent aim: the sense of tragedy: the sense of evil: the persuasion towards Adventure beyond achieved perfection; the sense of Peace" (AI 380). But Whitehead adds that the concept of civilization as developed to this point remains incomplete. No argument is available to determine what is fully required for civilization.

Whitehead says that the motto of every metaphysician should be the saying of Cardinal Newman: "*Non in dialectica complacuit Deo salvum facere populum suum*" (AI 380). Thus the metaphysician should understand that argument and counterargument will not allow us to reach the divine order of things. The great truths are beyond words, that is, beyond literal statement or reasoning. Civilization depends on an appetite for adventure, and, Whitehead says, "Adventure belongs to the essence of civilization" (AI 380). In like manner, speculative thought is the adventure of the mind. Such an extension of thought is necessary to civilization. Speculation is the essence of thought. Argument has its place but it does not take us beyond ourselves.

The ultimate opposition is between Plato's Receptacle, which is the stable element in all things, and Adventure, which includes Eros, the living urge toward all possibilities. Philosophy, with its speculative abilities, stands in the middle of this great opposition. It can neither restrain itself with the surety of argument nor allow itself to pass beyond the powers of reason to mere speculation without purpose and insight. Philosophy is civilized thought. In relation to the human condition, philosophy is our means to comprehend the great ideas of truth, beauty, art, adventure, and peace. In order to understand civilization we may consider each of these in turn.

Whitehead says, "Truth is a qualification which applies to Appearance alone. Reality is just itself, and it is nonsense to ask whether it be true or false. Truth is the conformation of Appearance to Reality" (AI 309). Metaphysics begins with the thought of "is" that, to be understood, must be opposed to "is not." "Is" cannot be purely indeterminate or it would be the same as "is not," as Hegel has shown in the equation of being and nothing. Thus appearance must be the real but cannot be the completely real. It is the real only as it shows itself. The pursuit of truth, that which results from the desire to know, is the pursuit of the connection between the real and its appearance. Whitehead says, "The two conspicuous examples of the truth-relation in human experience are afforded by propositions and by sense-perception" (AI 311–12).

No sentence merely states a proposition. It has always a subjective dimension that calls us to believe something, or doubt or obey. Whitehead says, "It is more important that a proposition be interesting than that it be true" (AI 313; see also PR 395–96). Truth adds interest. Interest is adventure at the level of logical thought. As Whitehead says in *The Aims of Education*, "A merely well-informed man is the most useless bore on God's earth."[2]

The other example of the truth-relation is one humans share with animals. "For animals on this Earth, sense-perception is the culmination of Appearance" (AI 314). Animals function on the level of appearance as the data of their sense perception. Reality is not a problem for them, nor is it for human beings, in the sense that any sense perception is what it is. Whitehead says, "Within any type of truth-relation a distinction arises. The Reality functions in the past, the Appearance is perceived in the present" (AI 317). A perception had in the past is a standard and a perception in the present is another appearance of it. Thus we can feel a kind of truth-relation on the level of perception.

Whitehead says, "There is a third type of truth-relation which is even vaguer and more indirect than the second type considered above. It may be termed the type of 'symbolic truth'" (AI 318). Whitehead holds that languages and their meanings are examples of this type, in the sense that there are right or wrong uses of any particular language among the speakers and writers of that language. "Music, ceremonial clothing, ceremonial smells, and ceremonial rhythmic visual appearances, also have symbolic truth, or symbolic falsehood" (AI 319). Symbolic truth depends on what is appropriate within the subjective feelings of a given community. An intended meaning is either properly embodied in a form of human expression or it is not. The wrong symbol can transgress the meaning of the human reality it attempts to represent. What Whitehead designates here as symbolic truth has a resonance with Cassirer's basisphenomenon of the work, in that the work is the objectification for other selves of what otherwise is contained within the subjective life of the self. What Whitehead regards as beauty also fits Cassirer's conception of the work.

Whitehead says that "Beauty is a wider, and more fundamental, notion than Truth" (AI 341). Truth concerns only the relations between

2. Whitehead, *Aims of Education*, 1.

appearance and reality, and it requires that these two factors of this opposition have something in common. Beauty has less restriction than this in bringing elements of experience together. Whitehead defines beauty as "the internal conformation of the various items of experience with each other, for the production of maximum effectiveness" (AI 341). We understand harmony through beauty. Truth can show us the connections between thoughts, perceptions, and symbols, but it is in beauty that we can experience harmony. Whitehead says, "Thus any part of experience can be beautiful. The teleology of the Universe is directed to the production of Beauty. Thus any system of things which in any wide sense is beautiful is to that extent justified in its existence" (AI 341). Systems of thought as well as systems of nature can be beautiful. In them we can experience perfection.

In Whitehead's enumeration of the ideas of civilization, missing is that of goodness or moral perfection. He includes goodness, to an extent, under the idea of beauty. He says, "Goodness is the third member of the trinity which traditionally has been assigned as the complex aim of art—namely, Truth, Beauty, and Goodness. With the point of view here adopted, Goodness must be denied a place among the aims of art. For Goodness is a qualification belonging to the constitution of reality, which in any of its individual actualizations is better or worse" (AI 345).

Truth and beauty are absolutes, perfections. There can be, strictly speaking, no relative "truth" or relative "beauty." One is reminded of the equation of the famous lines of Keats' "Ode on a Grecian Urn": "'Beauty is truth, truth beauty',—that is all / Ye know on earth, and all ye need to know." In Keats' equation, goodness is excluded. Or it is perhaps the hidden middle term of the syllogism that connects beauty to truth. Whatever is beautiful is good and whatever is true is also good. Whitehead says, "The real world is good when it is beautiful" (AI 345). Moral excellence or goodness when it is absolute is identical to both truth and beauty. If it is less than absolute, it is relative to conditions of the real as they bear on human action.

The good is different in kind from art because it is "a qualification belonging to the constitution of reality," whereas "art has essentially to do with perfections attainable by purposeful adaptation of appearance" (AI 345). Whitehead's implicit view is that when truth and beauty are pursued, goodness will occur in human affairs and consciousness, without the need for specific cultivation. Whitehead says, "Science and Art are the consciously determined pursuit of Truth and Beauty" (AI 350). This pursuit results in the establishment of the fundamental institutions of civilization. These two great ideas provide humanity with the senses of harmony necessary for civilized life.

Truth and beauty cannot alone account for the achievement of civilization. They must be joined to the idea of adventure. Whitehead says, "Adventure is essential, namely, the search for new perfections" (AI 332). Whitehead's concern is that civilization will be understood to depend solely upon the cultivation of the greatness of the past. Indeed, the consciousness of the West looks back to the golden age of Athens and to the revival of the arts and sciences of Renaissance Florence. Whitehead insists, however, that the future cannot be simply modeled on the past. We must realize that the great moments of civilization of the past are so because of their involvement with adventure. These moments come into existence only because of an adherence to adventure. Whitehead says, "Without adventure civilization is in full decay" (AI 360).

Societies that rigidly hold only to tradition allow human possibility to stagnate. They fail truly to understand the meaning of the past, how that which they wish to preserve perfectly came into being. Whitehead says, "Only the adventurous can understand the greatness of the past" (AI 360). The past must be always with us. It is the basis of human learning, but the past must be seen as a repository of possibilities for the future. It cannot be seen as the future itself.

Greatness requires the pursuit of harmony, in which the various fields of knowledge and dimensions of social activity act in concert. In this, Whitehead's view is in accord with Cassirer's view of the harmony of the symbolic forms. But to harmony, Whitehead holds, we must add the principle of individuality, a principle with which Cassirer would not disagree. The key to the great achievements of the West is its willingness to value individuality. Whitehead says, "The great Harmony is the harmony of enduring individualities, connected in the unity of a background. It is for this reason that the notion of freedom haunts the higher civilizations. For freedom, in any one of its many senses, is the claim for vigorous self-assertion" (AI 362). If we connect this conception of freedom to Cassirer's claim that human culture at its base is a process of self-liberation, we can conclude that a doctrine of individuality is crucial. The individual is a microcosm of the macrocosm of human culture.

Whitehead sees the tetralogy of truth, beauty, art, and adventure as held together by peace. In peace we are seeking a "Harmony of Harmonies."

Peace, Whitehead says, "comes as a gift." He says, "I choose the term 'Peace' for that Harmony of Harmonies which calms destructive turbulence and completes civilization" (AI 367). Peace is a more essential quality than love, Whitehead claims, because love is too narrow an idea, too tied to the particular personality. Love is a particularized sense of feeling, whereas peace "is a broadening of feeling due to the emergence of some deep metaphysical insight, unverbalized and yet momentous in its coordination of values" (AI 367).

In his discussion of these great ideas, Whitehead repeatedly returns to the importance of beauty. Beauty is a greater force for the experience of harmony than is truth, and it is a wider idea than art. Peace is an absolute sense of things that surpasses the relativity of values that is characteristic of personality. Peace, Whitehead holds, "is primarily a trust in the efficacy of Beauty" (AI 367).

Peace is the outcome of tragedy. "Peace is the understanding of tragedy, and at the same time its preservation" (AI 368). Whitehead says, "Each tragedy is the disclosure of an ideal:—What might have been, and was not: What can be. The tragedy was not in vain. . . . The inner feeling belonging to this grasp of the service of tragedy is Peace—the purification of the emotions" (AI 369). Catharsis results in peace. Whitehead could agree with the Spanish philosopher Miguel de Unamuno's theme of *el sentimiento trágico de la vida*, "the tragic sense of life," in its most general sense as a genuine part of human life, both in individuals and in peoples, but he would disagree with Unamuno's view that there is no resolution to tragedy.

Unamuno holds that we philosophize in order to live, in the sense of trying to resign ourselves to life or at least to distract ourselves from its griefs. Whitehead's view counters this view with the phenomenon of peace, for he says that peace is a positive feeling. This positive feeling is motivated by the sense of beauty. Truth is sustaining, but it is not ultimately sustaining. Beauty organizes the soul. The sense of harmony that beauty affords us leads to metaphysics. Because beauty shows us the meaning of harmony, Whitehead can so closely associate poetry and metaphysics.

Metaphysics is the attempt to make thought beautiful, to make reason take on to itself the sense of the harmony of harmonies that beauty shows to the senses and the emotions. Metaphysics is a kind of mental peace that results from the realization that the ideal of reason, the fully rational, is unreachable by the finitude of mind. Yet metaphysics is positive in the way that beauty is positive, and in the way that there is never perfect beauty.

The philosopher without an aesthetic sense can offer us only the flat line of literal-mindedness, the safety of the island of the understanding, closed off from reason.

The Function of Reason

In his lectures delivered at Princeton University in 1929, which appeared as the little volume *The Function of Reason*, Whitehead claims that there are two aspects of reason: "the Reason of Plato and the Reason of Ulysses, Reason as seeking a complete understanding and Reason seeking an immediate method of action."[3] Odysseus, or Ulysses, "the man of twists and turns driven time and again off course," grasps reason as an instrument, a means to get around in the world and accomplish an end. Reason is tied to survival. It can be used when needed. Of Plato and Ulysses, Whitehead says, "The one shares Reason with the Gods, the other with the foxes."[4] We could add to this Isaiah Berlin's distinction of the hedgehog and the fox. The hedgehog knows one big thing; the fox knows many things.

Goethe says of Plato that "Plato relates himself to the world as a blessed spirit, whom it pleases sometimes to stay for a while in the world; he is not so much concerned to come to know the world, because he already presupposes it, as to communicate to it in a friendly way what he brings along with him and what it needs. He penetrates into the depths more in order to fill them with his being than in order to investigate them. He moves longingly to the heights in order to become again part of his origin. . . . Plato, like an obelisk, indeed like a pointed flame, seeks heaven."[5]

Both senses of reason are distinctively human, and both are required for human life; that of Ulysses even to stay alive and that of Plato to supply the soul with its human vocation. From the reason of Ulysses comes *praxis* and from the reason of Plato comes *theoria*. *Theōrein* leads ultimately to speculation. Whitehead defines speculative philosophy as "the endeavour to frame a coherent, logical, necessary system of general ideas in terms of which every element of our experience can be interpreted. . . . The philosophical scheme should be coherent, logical, and in respect to its interpretation, applicable and adequate. Here 'applicable' means that some items of

3. Whitehead, *Function of Reason*, 11.

4. Ibid., 10.

5. Quoted by Cassirer, "The Concept of Philosophy as a Philosophical Problem," in *Symbol, Myth, and Culture*, 50–51.

experience are thus interpretable, and 'adequate' means that there are no items incapable of such interpretation" (PR 4).

There are, then, four primary properties that adhere to speculative philosophy—coherence, logical necessity, applicability, and adequacy. Coherence is the principle that the fundamental ideas of the speculative scheme presuppose each other. They are a system of interrelations whose meaning is connected to the place they occupy in the totality. Logical necessity is essentially the adherence to the law of non-contradiction. The system of ideas cannot affirm both A and non-A, taking A in both instances in the same sense. The principle of logical necessity in this conception simply means that the system cannot be irrational. But Whitehead's conception of speculative philosophy and the categorical scheme that he advances are generally missing a sense of dialectic.

Although process is at the heart of his system, Whitehead's methodology is analogous to that of "working hypotheses" as they are connected to theories (AI 283). Whitehead's metaphysics has a version of what Hegel calls "determinate negation," that is, that the negative of anything has content and is not simply a null class. But Whiteheadian metaphysics offers us no logic of process. Process is described, but the opposites of the law of non-contradiction are not converted into contraries such that non-A is a development of A. In Whitehead's system we are able to *think about* process, but we are not given a definite means to *think* process. Whitehead sees speculative philosophy as an extension of scientific thinking rather than as a mode of thinking that itself passes beyond theory and its application to evidence. For all of his awareness of the importance of art and beauty, Whitehead seems unable to enter into the inner form of actuality itself— like the poet. This would require metaphysical thought to become musical instead of theoretical.

Whitehead's requirements of applicability and adequacy, he says, are the empirical side of speculative thought. To speculate is not simply to turn thought in upon itself, unconnected to the world. The purpose of speculation is ultimately to explain the world in theoretical terms that are connected to facts. Regarding facts, no one is more aware than Whitehead that facts are through and through structured by theory. Whitehead holds that no fact is simply a fact, a such-and-such. Moreover, that there are facts is itself a theory of the world. Whitehead says, "The main method of philosophy in dealing with its evidence is that of descriptive generalization" (AI 301). The requirement of necessity is not exhausted by that to be found in formal logic. It applies to the aim of speculative philosophy to secure in thought what is truly universal in human experience and hence in reality, of which humanity and its institutions are a part. Whitehead says, "Thus the philosophic scheme should be 'necessary,' in the sense of bearing in itself its own warrant of universality throughout all experience, provided that we confine ourselves to that which communicates with immediate matter of fact" (PR 5). There is an essence to the universe and this essence is open to rationality. It is this essence that speculative philosophy seeks.

The philosopher, like the poet but unlike the scientist, has only language available as the means of thought. In addition to language, the scientist has experiment and all that it entails captured in the understanding of the "scientific method." There are no experiments in the scientific sense that can be performed in metaphysics. Open to the metaphysician are so-called thought experiments, but such a process of reasoning is always logically a *petitio principii*, for they must assume what they intend to prove. However, the thought experiment as a phenomenological exercise engaged in to make evident a metaphysical point can greatly increase comprehension of it. In the broadest sense, Whitehead's speculative scheme is a thought experiment of the first order. It, like all metaphysical systems, is a tautology.

Whitehead rightly emphasizes that metaphysical first principles can never be fully written down. He says, "Philosophers can never hope finally to formulate these metaphysical first principles. Weakness of insight and deficiencies of language stand in the way inexorably" (PR 6). Whitehead is both Socratic and Platonic in his conception of the relation of philosophy to language. He says that speculative philosophy must take ordinary meanings of words and attempt to extend them into new meanings without simply inventing a technical vocabulary. Even though Whitehead's categorical scheme appears, at first encounter, to be a welter of technical words, the rest of the text of *Process and Reality* is an attempt to show how the meanings of these terms have their roots in existing vocabulary in the history of philosophy as well as in common sense.

Whitehead's approach to the philosophical use of language, then, is like that of Socrates' attempts to speak the language of the *agora* but to extend its meanings to approach the philosophical insights he wishes to convey. Whitehead's approach to language is Platonic in the sense that it is aligned with Plato's famous assertion, in the *Seventh Letter*, that he never wrote down his philosophy. Plato, the greatest writer of dialogues in the history of human thought, can take us toward only a noetic grasp of the doctrine of forms and the meanings of the seven great ideas that Whitehead enumerates from the Platonic corpus.

Whitehead observes that "it has been remarked that a system of philosophy is never refuted; it is only abandoned" (PR 9). This may also be claimed of theories generally. Theories in science are replaced by other theories. It is a well-known point in the history of science that a theory may have problematic parts and be found defective in relation to specific pieces of evidence. But for the theory to be abandoned fully, a more adequate theoretical account of the issues involved must appear. No philosophy, however, simply claims just to be yet another philosophy.

A philosophy, especially a metaphysics, claims to have taken thought to the point of something that is absolute. This is the problem with the doctrine of pluralism. We may assume a general position of regarding various philosophies in relation to each other and assert a kind of relativism, saying that no philosophy appears to be final. But the motivation for pursuing philosophy is to find the true and the real. Otherwise one is only a commentator on philosophies, or a skeptic. Any philosophy that pursues the absolute necessarily claims to answer skepticism. This pursuit of the absolute need not entail the view that all other philosophical systems are in error. Instead it may rightly take the position that "the bundle of philosophic systems expresses a variety of general truths about the universe, awaiting co-ordination and assignment of their various spheres of validity. Such progress in co-ordination is provided by the advance of philosophy; and in this sense philosophy has advanced from Plato onwards" (PR 11).

We encounter this view in Aristotle, in his discussion of his predecessors in founding his metaphysics. We encounter it again, in a new form, in Pico della Mirandola's attempt at the "syncretism" of the truths of diverse philosophies. And we find it, above all, in Hegel's conception of the history of philosophy as a continual development of the idea. The production of new philosophy cannot do without the history of philosophy, and the history of philosophy must be philosophically, not simply historically, understood.

It is rightly said that language is never left the same after the appearance of a great work of literature. The same may be said of philosophical thought, as it is never left the same after the appearance of a great philosophy. "Philosophy never reverts to its old position after the shock of a great philosopher" (PR 16). Whitehead's principle of adventure applies to philosophy itself, because "the study of philosophy is a voyage towards the larger generalities" (PR 14). It is these larger generalities that take philosophy and human knowledge beyond the confines of the particular sciences, although these generalities must always reflect what can be known in a specific use of reason and empirical investigation.

Since the Platonic instruction that, to enter the Academy, a knowledge of mathematics was required, metaphysics has had a close involvement with mathematics. Within his own career, Whitehead is both mathematician and metaphysician. But he is clear that philosophy is not to be pursued as a kind of mathematical reasoning. More broadly put, philosophy cannot be confined to the application of symbolic or mathematical logic to problems of the nature of knowledge and the real. Whitehead says, "The primary method of mathematics is deduction; the primary method of philosophy is descriptive generalization. Under the influence of mathematics, deduction has been foisted onto philosophy as its standard method, instead of taking its true place as an essential auxiliary mode of verification whereby to test the scope of generalities" (PR 15–16).

Whitehead's claim is parallel to that of the higher stages of the Platonic Divided Line. For thought to pursue the absolute (the Platonic Good) to its end, it must pass beyond the stage of the "mathematicals," the *ta mathēmatica* to the *eidē* and *noēsis*. The voyage of thought is taken toward insight into first principles by its involvement with adventure. With adventure finally comes peace, in the form of contemplation, the state of mind necessary to speculative philosophy. Philosophy shares the ideal of peace with civilization. Metaphysics at this summit of thought has a sense of intellectual beauty, a harmony of harmonies that it first encounters at the level of mathematical order. Peace gives both thought and civilization a new lease on life. Here there is the realization that truth cannot be captured in the precision of the proposition. Language must always be seen as a process in which meaning goes beyond it. "The position of metaphysics in the development of culture cannot be understood without remembering that no verbal statement is the adequate expression of a proposition" (PR 20). But the language of speculative reason is more than the attempt to formulate true propositions. It is the fulfillment of the imagination to reach the whole, to reach the really real.

We can conclude that Whitehead's conception of speculative philosophy is twofold. It is metaphysics in the literal sense of the word—the formation of hypotheses of higher generality than those that can be treated by physics—and thus is a kind of thinking that comes after the limits of physics have been reached. The result is metaphysics as cosmology, and it is reflected in the subtitle of *Process and Reality—An Essay in Cosmology*. It is also metaphysics in the greatest sense of the word—the attempt by the mind to extend reason and imagination to their fullest powers and attempt a complete speech of the real, of things divine and human—the ultimate Platonic "likely story" that takes place when thought has exhausted its ordinary, dialectical, comparative, and argumentative modes of understanding and decides to pass beyond them.

Actual Entities

Whitehead's theory of reality has as its center one idea—that of "actual entities." They are, Whitehead says, "the final real things of which the world is made up. There is no going behind actual entities to find anything more real. They differ among themselves: God is an actual entity, and so is the most trivial puff of existence in far-off empty space" (PR 27–28). If we alter the middle term in the title of *Process and Reality* from a conjunction to a verb, we have the essence of Whitehead's "cosmological metaphysics"—process is reality. Whitehead says, "The notion of 'substance' is transformed into that of 'actual entity'" (PR 28). At the basis of all things is not substance or any sense of prime matter but process, activity, constant self-transformation. Whitehead says, of the actual entity, "Its 'being' is constituted by its 'becoming.' This is the 'principle of process'" (PR 34–35).

Dorothy Emmet, one of the early and best interpreters of Whitehead's metaphysics, remarked that Whitehead's system might best benefit from philosophers speaking of it in their own way, rather than becoming completely enmeshed in the interconnections of the technical terminology of its categorical scheme.[6] However, when one turns to the many works of interpretation of Whitehead's thought, this scholastic discussion and analysis is largely what one finds. My purpose in these remarks is to take a middle way in order to comprehend in essence what I take to be Whitehead's most original metaphysical insight.

Whitehead's technical term, "actual entity," describes what we would ordinarily think of as a subject or a self. The meanings of the complex terminology of Whitehead's categorical scheme are to a large extent defined in terms of each other, much as can be done in mathematics or formal deductive systems. But Whitehead does not intend this to be the only or even the

6. Emmet, "Whitehead, Alfred North," 294–95.

best way they can be understood. He regards his terminology as extensions and precisions of meanings that already exist in philosophical language and in ordinary speech. In discussing the process of feeling, a basic way in which actual entities participate in the world, he says, "A feeling cannot be abstracted from the actual entity entertaining it. This actual entity is termed the 'subject' of the feeling" (PR 338). Actual entities must be more than constructs. They must truly be entities, if we are to avoid what Whitehead calls the "fallacy of misplaced concreteness" (PR 11).

Whitehead says he has retained the term "subject" because it is familiar in philosophy, but he says the term "superject" should be added to it, thus: "subject-superject." These two terms together describe an actual entity in that, as subject, it builds itself up by taking into itself data. The subject has purpose in its self-process; its activity is oriented toward a final cause. When its data are so formed and it becomes an object available for other actual entities, it attains its superject status. It has, so to speak, finished its career. Its immortality is achieved in the formation of itself to the point of the superject.

Whitehead says, "All actual entities share with God this characteristic of self-causation. For this reason every actual entity also shares with God the characteristic of transcending all other actual entities, including God. The universe is thus a creative advance into novelty" (PR 339–40). Each actual entity is a completely unique reality, a reality that it makes for itself. In so doing it transcends all other realities, including God, who is also an actual entity. But actual entities live lives, and at the point of their superject nature, they perish. They live on, in the appropriation of their reality as incorporated into the internal process of self-creation by other actual entities. The superject phase of the actual entity is analogous to the basisphenomen of the work in Cassirer's analysis of the self, in which the achievement of the self in the work is also a loss of the self to other selves.

The actual entity is an analogue to the ordinary process by which I become a human self. Whitehead explains this process in a well-known passage in *Modes of Thought*: "I shape the activities of the environment into a new creation, which is myself at this moment; and yet, as being myself, it is a continuation of the antecedent world. If we stress the role of the environment, this process is causation. If we stress the role of my immediate pattern of active enjoyment, this process is self-creation. If we stress the role of the conceptual anticipation of the future whose existence is a necessity in the nature of the present, this process is the teleological aim at some ideal in the future."[7] The creation of the human self is always a process of past, present, and future. A human self is an actual entity writ large.

Whitehead must account for the three things that Descartes and Kant bequeath to modern philosophy—the reality of the self, the world, and God. The actual entity accounts for the world by accounting for the self in it. Whitehead, as mentioned, accounts for God as an actual entity. The special problems connected with the sense of God as an actual entity will be discussed in the next section.

Whitehead's second unique metaphysical conception is what he calls "prehension." He says, "That every prehension consists of three factors: (*a*) the 'subject' which is prehending, namely, the actual entity in which that prehension is a concrete element; (*b*) the 'datum' which is prehended; (*c*) the 'subjective' forms which is *how* that subject prehends that datum" (PR 35). Actual entities have a mental and a physical pole. Thus when an actual entity prehends an idea it is an instance of "conceptual prehension," and when it reacts to the presence of another actual entity that is thus for it a datum, it is an instance of "physical prehension." These physical prehensions are the content of the physical pole, as those conceptual prehensions are the content of the mental pole. The process of incorporating data into the life of the actual entity is "concrescence."

Whitehead's replacement of substance with subject calls to mind Hegel's sentence in the *Phenomenology*, that "the living Substance is being which is in truth *Subject*, or, what is the same, is in truth actual only in so far as it is the movement of positing itself, or is the mediation of its self-othering with itself" (PS 18; 20). Hegel asserts this equation as true of human consciousness, whereas Whitehead projects it as a cosmological principle. Whitehead also could subscribe to Hegel's claim that the "True is the whole." Both are philosophers of organism as the root metaphor of their metaphysics. Both are against what Whitehead calls "vacuous actuality"—actuality that has no inner life.

Even more, Whitehead's doctrine of actual entities calls to mind Leibniz's metaphysics of monads. In *Science and the Modern World*, Whitehead makes this connection clear. He says, "It is obvious that the basing of philosophy upon the presupposition of organism must be traced back to Leibniz. His monads are for him the ultimately real entities." Leibniz was unable fully to transcend substance metaphysics. He faced the need to combine two points of view. One was to hold that the real was an activity

---

7. Whitehead, *Modes of Thought*, 228.

internally organizing itself into a unity through a system of internal relations. The other was that real entities are substances with inhering properties with relations among such substances being accidental to their reality.
Whitehead says, "To combine these two points of view, his monads were
therefore windowless; and their passions merely mirrored the universe by
the divine arrangement of a preëstablished harmony."[8] Leibniz was unable
to turn being into a total process of becoming that is embodied in the living organism. Whitehead's principle of prehension, then, guarantees that
actual entities are living, organic processes.

Whitehead has no need for a doctrine of pre-established harmony
because actual entities, in their activity of prehending, can form a nexus.
He says, "A nexus is a set of actual entities in the unity of the relatedness
constituted by their prehensions of each other, or—what is the same thing,
conversely expressed—constituted by their objectifications in each other"
(PR 35). Nexus is the most primitive sense of society or community. From
this general power of association through prehension, society in every
sense of the word develops.

We may add to Whitehead's theories of actual entities and prehensions a third theory, that of eternal objects. We will then have at least a
working outline of the basis of his metaphysics. Whitehead's eternal objects
are intended to account for what is thought to be universal in experience.
They are Plato's ideas, or the categories of philosophical idealism. Whitehead says, "An eternal object can be described only in terms of its potentiality for 'ingression' into the becoming of actual entities; and that its analysis
only discloses other eternal objects. It is a pure potential" (PR 34). The
actual entities are particulars. Eternal objects are universals. By conceiving
universals as eternal objects, and their function as pure potentiality, Whitehead intends to avoid the Platonic problem of how the forms participate
in things. Once substance has become subject it is capable of allowing the
"ingression" of the universal into its process of self-development.

The universal is a potential to be realized in its activity. Whitehead
says, "An eternal object is always a potentiality for actual entities; but in
itself, as conceptually felt, it is neutral as to the fact of its physical ingression
in any particular actual entity of the temporal world" (PR 70). The aim, in
the particular actual entity attaching itself to the universality of the eternal
object, is an attempt at being more than a fleeting existent. One way to
put this is that every actual entity is seeking being, in the sense of its own

8. Whitehead, *Science and the Modern World*, chap. 9.

immortality. Nothing is purely given for it. It desires to terminate its be-coming in the being of all that there is. Thus: "The actual entity terminates its becoming in one complex feeling involving a completely determinate bond with every item in the universe, the bond being either a positive or a negative prehension. This termination is the 'satisfaction' of the actual entity."

If we put this in terms of Whitehead's philosophy of civilization, the adventure that governs the life of becoming of the actual entity results in peace. Peace means that the actual entity finds its place in the world, because its place is an achievement. It has no nature that is given to it. Whitehead says, "This is the doctrine of the emergent unity of the superject. An actual entity is to be conceived both as a subject presiding over its own imme-diacy of becoming and a superject which is the atomic creature exercising its function of objective immortality." The actual entity makes itself what it is by both positively prehending what it wishes and negatively prehending what it wishes to exclude from its being. But when it is finished with this process, which includes the ingression of eternal objects, it attains the peace of its satisfaction. "It has become a 'being'; and it belongs to the future of every 'being' that it is a potential for every 'becoming.'"

The natural death of an actual entity is the point at which it ceases to be a subject and becomes the superject of its own making. It accomplishes this attainment in its own way. Thus: "This doctrine, that the final 'satisfac-tion' of an actual entity is intolerant of any addition, expresses the fact that every actual entity—since it is what it is—is finally its own reason for what it omits" (PR 71). The actuality of its own death, having manifested its su-perject nature, becomes a potentiality for the prehension of the becoming of the universe of actual entities at that moment. Since the superject is more than a fleeting state of the subject, it requires the universality of the eternal object to be realized in it. Sheer particularity offers no meaning and hence offers no possibility of satisfaction.

Whiteheadian metaphysics is ultimately a portrait of the self, speaking to itself about the self. Constantly, throughout *Process and Reality*, there is a search for a way to put this speech into words. The terms which initially appear only technical come to take on a life of their own. But it is a lan-guage that can be spoken only to those who have crossed the threshold of Whitehead's speculative reason. What Whitehead says would be incompre-hensible to the twists and turns of the reason of Ulysses. Ulysses fascinates us with his ability to solve problems, to know exactly what is called for in each and every situation. But once home in Ithaca, and having overcome the suitors and regained his royal residence, tragedy avoided, his adventure ends in restful peace. It will be centuries until Plato sets reason to work on the narrations of Homer and invents the idea that there are ideas, transposing adventure from the voyaging of the world to the voyaging of the mind. Tragedy becomes the subject of art and contemplation becomes the peace provided to the psyche. Whitehead has both of these figures in his conception of the actual entity: the constant movement and purpose of Ulysses and the stability and permanence of the eternal objects of Plato.

Final Interpretation

Whitehead's speculative cosmology contains a natural theology. We come, finally, to the question of God and the world. Whitehead's concern is not to prove the existence of God but to show how God can be included in the order of actual entities. In his lectures published as *Religion in the Making*, given in 1926, just prior to his Gifford Lectures in 1927–28 that were to become *Process and Reality*, Whitehead said, "God is that non-temporal actuality which has to be taken account of in every creative phase."[9] It is clear from what has been said of Whitehead's conception of reality that God is not to be understood as a being transcendent of the world. Instead the question is one of how God can be in the world and yet not of the world, not simply an aspect of the world's existence.

Aristotle, from the standpoint of his substance metaphysics, states the problem: "If, then, God is always in that good state in which we sometimes are, this compels our wonder; and if in a better this compels it yet more. And God *is* in a better state. And life also belongs to God; for the actuality of thought is life, and God is that actuality; and God's essential actuality is life most good and eternal. We say therefore that God is a living being, eternal, most good, so that life and duration continuous and eternal belong to God; for this *is* God" (*Metaph.* 1072b). God must be an actuality that does not perish and that thus is both alive and eternal. Furthermore, God's actuality must be in some sense not God's alone, but stand in some relation to the world.

On the ultimate order of the universe, Aristotle says, "We must consider also in which of two ways the nature of the universe contains the good or the highest good, whether as something separate and by itself, or as the

---

9. Whitehead, *Religion in the Making*, 91.

order of the parts. Probably in both ways, as an army does. For the good is found both in the order and in the leader, and more in the latter; for he does not depend on the order but it depends on him. And all things are ordered together somehow, but not all alike,—both fishes and fowls and plants; and the world is not such that one thing has nothing to do with another, but they are connected. For all are ordered together to one end" (*Metaph.* 1075a).

Aristotle's analogy of the leader of an army suggests that any ultimate principle of actuality or entity is both something in itself, and yet what it is to itself must have content in the sense that it must find itself in the parts of which it is the unity. To think of God as an absolute other is to think of an actuality that is sheer novelty, which is oblivion. To be in any meaningful sense is to be in relation to something. That something may be another aspect in some sense of itself. Otherwise we could not think of the absolute or God as self-caused.

We may add, to these metaphysical requirements of God, the cosmological view of God as maker of the universe. In the *Timaeus* Plato speaks of the demiurge or *dēmiourgos*, who brings order to the world, using the Forms or Ideas as patterns, seeing physical things as within a "receptacle" onto which these patterns are imposed. The receptacle, as Whitehead says, is one of the seven great ideas of Plato. In some sense God must function as maker of all that there is. As Timaeus says, "Now as to the whole universe [*Ouranos*] or world order (cosmos)—let's just call it by whatever name is most acceptable in a given context—there is a question we need to consider first. This is the sort of question one should begin with in inquiring into any subject. Has it always existed? Was there no origin from which it came to be? Or did it come to be and take its start from some origin?" (*Tim.* 28b).

These are ancient questions, and, as Whitehead says in his account of "God and the World," "We must not expect simple answers to far-reaching questions. However far our gaze penetrates, there are always heights beyond which block our vision" (PR 519). Whitehead's picture of God as demiurge is summed up in his attribution to God of both a consequent and a primordial nature. He claims, "Thus, analogously to all actual entities, the nature of God is dipolar. He has a primordial nature and a consequent nature. The consequent nature of God is conscious; and it is the realization of the actual world in the unity of his nature, and through the transformation of his wisdom. The primordial nature is conceptual, the consequent nature is the weaving of God's physical feelings upon his primordial concepts" (PR 524).

God unites form and matter within his own actuality. God is the cosmic receptacle in this sense.

God and the world are opposites, yet, as Whitehead says, "Opposed elements stand for each other in mutual requirement. In their unity, they inhibit or contrast." What is true, then, of any pair of opposites is true of God and the world. "God and the World stand to each other in this opposed requirement. God is the infinite ground of all mentality, the unity of vision seeking physical multiplicity. The World is the multiplicity of finites, actualities seeking a perfected unity." Multiplicity and unity seek each other in terms of both the mental and physical poles of God as actual entity. God's actuality includes the world. "Neither God, nor the World, reaches static completion. Both are in the grip of the ultimate metaphysical ground, the creative advance into novelty. Either of them, God and the World, is the instrument of novelty for the other" (PR 529).

Creative advance into novelty takes place in terms of the exchange between opposites. God's relation to the world is not static. If it were, God would be transcendent from the world once God created the world. This would be possible in terms of a substance metaphysics. But the metaphysics of process requires that the world not only has a constant connection to God but that God has a constant involvement with the world. The question arises: If the world and God are aspects of each other within the same actuality, is God in fact the world, and the reverse? If this is so in some sense, process metaphysics is a version of pantheism. I do not think that a doctrine of pantheism is the result of God's status as an actual entity. Instead, I think the result is a doctrine of panentheism, namely, that God includes the world as a part, though not the whole, of his being.

God is in all of the world in the creative advance into novelty, but not in each actual entity of the world in the same way and to the same extent. God has a superject nature because he provides data to be prehended in the self-creative activity of other actual entities. The superject nature of God is what distinguishes God as an actual entity from other actual entities and which affords these actual entities access to the actuality of God. God in his superject nature becomes not only the basis for creative advance into novelty but the basis of harmony in the universe in God's power to prehend all other actual entities. God, then, is the source of beauty in the universe and also the source of peace that comes from surmounting the tragedy of loss in the continual perishing of the particular actual entities as they complete their lives.

The problematic nature of the principles of any metaphysics always is most evident at the point of what it claims to be ultimate reality. Whitehead is quite aware of this, as he makes clear that his purpose is to explain dispassionately how the principles of his metaphysics apply to God. He says, "There is nothing here in the nature of proof." He also makes clear that "God is not to be treated as an exception to all metaphysical principles, invoked to save their collapse. He is their chief exemplification" (PR 521). He has avoided the problems of God as an unmoved mover, transcendent of creation yet regarded as its cause. He has further, through his doctrine of prehension, overcome the problem of the Leibnizian monadology in which God must in some sense have the ability to act as an external cause on the world, despite the fact that all monads, including God, act only in terms of cause as internal to their reality.

The central question that the reader faces, at the end of *Process and Reality*, is that God as an actual entity, unlike all other actual entities, does not perish! There can be no death of God. God's immortality is infinite, not finite. God's existence as an actual entity does not terminate with the presence of his developed superject nature. Other actual entities achieve immortality when their existence is prehended and preserved in the actuality of other actual entities. All actual entities can prehend God's superject nature, and God's existence is thus preserved *for them* in so doing. But God also has the power to preserve his own immortality. God is omnipotent in this regard.

A second question, raised in some of the literature, is God's "religious availability" in terms of Whitehead's conception. Whitehead is clear that his conception of God is purely metaphysical and is not intended as a reflection of any particular religious doctrine. One certainly does not perceive Whitehead's God as an entity to answer prayers (although prayer might be conceived as an avenue to God's concrescence), or around which to organize religious worship or ceremonies (although these two are not precluded by God's relation to the world). If religion is considered in Whitehead's own terms, I think, the "religious availability" problem is eliminated or greatly reduced. Whitehead says, "Religion is what the individual does with his solitariness."[10] Religion requires exactly what metaphysics requires—contemplation. Contemplation is inherently a religious act because it is only through contemplation that we can reach a sense of the ultimate and peace.

10. Ibid., 47.

Since, for Whitehead, thought is not opposed to feeling, metaphysics and religion are forms of our inner life. For Whitehead, religion is not a social activity, and neither is metaphysical thought. Philosophy may involve friendship, in the sense that Socrates asks questions in the *agora*, but these questions originate in the solitariness for which Socrates is also famous. In like manner, Whitehead acknowledges the value of the insights of the great world religions, but the meaning of these insights requires the individual to absorb them in solitariness. The point is not to dissolve religion and metaphysics into each other. It is still true, on this view, as Hegel holds, that religious thought is tied to *Vorstellungen* and metaphysics to speculative reason. But they both require the same state of the soul for their origination and continuance.

As Aristotle, in Book Lambda of the *Metaphysics*, quoted above, resorts to images to grasp the connection of God to the world, so Whitehead quite deliberately also does. Whitehead says, "The image—and it is but an image—the image under which this operative growth of God's nature [the creative advance into novelty] is best conceived, is that of tender care that nothing be lost. . . . He saves the world as it passes into the immediacy of his own life" (PR 525). A further sense in which God saves the world is his function as the repository of the eternal objects that is crucial to his role as demiurge. "Thus the many eternal objects conceived in their bare isolated multiplicity lack any consistent character. They require the transition to the conception of them as efficaciously existent by reason of God's conceptual realization of them" (PR 530). As curator of the eternal objects, God is the ultimate agency of all thought.

Whitehead's God is transhistorical. We are relieved, by the existence of God and God's presence in the world, of the "terror of history" that was discussed earlier. Whitehead says, "The world is thus faced by the paradox that, at least in its higher actualities, it craves for novelty and yet is haunted by terror at the loss of the past, with its familiarities and its loved ones. It seeks escape from time in its character of 'perpetually perishing'" (PR 516). Without metaphysical insight into the divine, human beings are left in history without any objective ground for freedom developed through self-determination. Metaphysics as well as religion are the means to confront time. The novelty of the future must be offset by the memory of the past. The life of actual entities, like the complex life of the self, moves between these two limits.

Whitehead's final image in *Process and Reality* is that "God is the great companion—the fellow-sufferer who understands" (PR 532). Speculative philosophy takes us to this final image. It is the peace that contemplation can provide. The solitariness that thought provides takes us out of the time of ongoing events and into the great time of origin. This is the time where all is possible and the patience of the divine resides. The self can thus preserve itself and draw upon its inner from. This self-preservation is a divine moment in the face of vicissitude.

Bibliography

Editions that appear in the List of Abbreviations and Citations do not appear in the Bibliography.

Anselm, St. *Basic Writings.* Translated by S. W. Deane. LaSalle, IL: Open Court, 1962.

Apel, Karl-Otto. *Die Idee der Sprache in der Tradition des Humanismus von Dante bis Vico.* Bonn: Bouvier Verlag Herbert Grundmann, 1975.

Bacon, Francis. "Of Vicissitude of Things." In *The Major Works,* edited by Brian Vickers, 451–54. New York: Oxford University Press, 2002.

Berkeley, George. *Three Dialogues between Hylas and Philonous.* New York: Bobbs-Merrill, 1954.

Bloch, Ernst. "Zerstörte Sprache—zerstörte Kultur." In *Deutsche Literatur im Exil 1933–1945: Texte und Dokumente,* edited by Michael Winkler, 353–54. Stuttgart: Reclam, 1979.

Borges, Jorge Luis. "The Immortal." In *Collected Fictions,* translated by Andrew Hurley, 183–95. New York: Penguin, 1999.

Bruno, Giordano. *The Ash Wednesday Supper.* Edited and translated by Edward A. Gosselin and Lawrence S. Lerner. Toronto: University of Toronto Press, 1995.

———. *Cause, Principle and Unity.* Translated by Robert de Lucca. Cambridge: Cambridge University Press, 1998.

———. *The Expulsion of the Triumphant Beast.* Translated by Arthur D. Imerti. Lincoln: University of Nebraska Press, 2004.

———. *On the Infinite Universe and Worlds.* Translated by Dorothea Waley Singer. New York: H. Schuman, 1950.

Cassirer, Ernst. "The Concept of Group and the Theory of Perception." Translated by Aron Gurwitsch. *Philosophy and Phenomenological Research* 5 (1944) 1–35.

———. *Das Erkenntnisproblem in der Philosophie und Wissenschaft der neueren Zeit.* Vols. 2–5 of *Gesammelte Werke.* Hamburg: Meiner, 1999.

———. *An Essay on Man: An Introduction to a Philosophy of Human Culture.* New Haven: Yale University Press, 1944.

———. *The Individual and the Cosmos in Renaissance Philosophy.* Translated by Mario Domandi. New York: Harper, 1963.

———. "The Influence of Language upon the Development of Scientific Thought." *Journal of Philosophy* 38 (1942) 309–27.

———. *Language and Myth.* Translated by Susanne K. Langer. New York: Dover, 1953.

———. *The Philosophy of the Enlightenment.* Translated by Fritz C. A. Koelln and James P. Pettegrove. Boston: Beacon, 1960.

――――. *The Problem of Knowledge: Philosophy, Science, and History since Hegel.* Translated by William H. Woglom and Charles W. Hendel. New Haven: Yale University Press, 1950.

――――. "'Spirit' and 'Life' in Contemporary Philosophy." In *The Philosophy of Ernst Cassirer,* edited by Paul Arthur Schilpp, 857–80. Evanston, IL: Library of Living Philosophers, 1949.

――――. *Substance and Function; and Einstein's Theory of Relativity.* Translated by William Curtis Swabey and Marie Collins Swabey. New York: Dover, 1953.

――――. *Symbol, Myth, and Culture: Essays and Lectures of Ernst Cassirer, 1935–1945.* Edited by Donald Phillip Verene. New Haven: Yale University Press, 1979.

――――. *The Warburg Years (1919–1933): Essays on Language, Art, Myth, and Technology.* Translated by S. G. Lofts and A. Calcagno. New Haven: Yale University Press, 2013.

Chroust, Anton-Hermann. *Aristotle's Protrepticus: A Reconstruction.* Notre Dame: University of Notre Dame Press, 1964.

Collingwood, R. G. *An Essay on Metaphysics.* Oxford: Clarendon, 1957.

――――. *An Essay on Philosophical Method.* Oxford: Clarendon, 1950.

Cornford, F. M. *From Religion to Philosophy: A Study in the Origins of Western Speculation.* New York: Harper, 1957.

――――. *Principium Sapientiae: The Origins of Greek Philosophical Thought.* Edited by W. K. C. Guthrie. New York: Harper, 1965.

Descartes, René. *Correspondance III: Janvier 1640–Juin 1643.* Vol. 3 of *Oeuvres de Descartes.* Edited by Charles Adam and Paul Tannery. Paris: Vrin, 1996.

――――. *Meditationes de Prima Philosophia.* Vol. 7 of *Oeuvres de Descartes.* Edited by Charles Adam and Paul Tannery. Paris: Vrin, 1996.

Eliade, Mircea, *The Myth of the Eternal Return.* Translated by Willard R. Trask. Princeton: Princeton University Press, 2005.

Emmet, Dorothy M. "Whitehead, Alfred North." In *The Encyclopedia of Philosophy,* edited by Paul Edwards, 8:294–95. New York: Macmillan, 1967.

Goethe, Johann Wolfgang von. *Maximen und Reflexionen.* Edited by Max Hecker. Schriften der Goethe- Gesellschaft 21. Weimar: Verlag der Goethe-Gesellschaft, 1907.

Gordon, Peter E. *Continental Divide: Heidegger, Cassirer, Davos.* Cambridge: Harvard University Press, 2010.

Gottschalk, H. B. *Heraclides of Pontus.* Oxford: Clarendon, 1980.

Grassi, Ernesto. *Rhetoric as Philosophy: The Humanist Tradition.* Translated by John Michael Krois and Azizeh Azodi. Carbondale: Southern Illinois University Press, 2001.

Guicciardini, Francesco. *Ricordi.* Milan: Rizzoli, 1977.

Hartshorne, Charles. *The Logic of Perfection and Other Essays in Neoclassical Metaphysics.* LaSalle, IL: Open Court, 1962.

Hegel, G. W. F. *Aesthetics: Lectures on Fine Art.* Translated by T. M. Knox. 2 vols. Oxford: Clarendon, 1975.

――――. *Briefe von und an Hegel.* Edited by Johannes Hoffmeister. Vol. 1, *1785–1812.* Hamburg: Meiner, 1952.

――――. "Das älteste Systemprogramm des deutschen Idealismus." In *Frühe Schriften,* vol. 1 of *Werke,* 234–36. Frankfurt am Main: Suhrkamp, 1986.

――――. "The 'Earliest System-Programme of German Idealism.'" In *Hegel's Development: Toward the Sunlight, 1770–1801,* by H. S. Harris, 510–12. Oxford: Clarendon, 1972.

————. *Lectures on the Philosophy of Religion*. Translated by R. F. Brown et al. 2 vols. Berkeley: University of California Press, 1984.

————. *The Logic of Hegel: The Encyclopaedia of the Philosophical Sciences*. Translated by William Wallace. Oxford: Oxford University Press, 1959.

————. "Die Religion der Erhabenheit." In *Vorlesungen über die Philosophie der Religion*, vol. 17 of *Werke*, 50–96. Frankfurt am Main: Suhrkamp, 1969.

Inwood, Michael James. *A Hegel Dictionary*. Oxford: Blackwell, 1992.

Kant, Immanuel. *Critique of Pure Reason*. Translated by Norman Kemp Smith. London: Macmillan, 1958.

Kline, George L. "Some Recent Reinterpretations of Hegel's Philosophy." *Monist* 48 (1964) 34–75.

Le Dœuff, Michèle. *The Philosophical Imaginary*. Translated by Colin Gordon. Stanford: Stanford University Press, 1989.

Lévi-Strauss, Claude. *The Raw and the Cooked: Introduction to a Science of Mythology*. Translated by John Weightman and Doreen Weightman. New York: Harper, 1969.

————. *The Savage Mind*. Chicago: University of Chicago Press, 1966.

Mercanton, Jacques. "The Hours of James Joyce." Translated by Lloyd C. Parks. In *Portraits of the Artist in Exile: Recollections of James Joyce by Europeans*, edited by Willard Potts, 205–52. New York: Harcourt Brace Jovanovich, 1986.

Mueller, Gustav E. "The Hegel Legend of 'Thesis-Antithesis-Synthesis.'" *Journal of the History of Ideas* 19 (1958) 411–14.

Nicholas of Cusa. *Nicholas of Cusa on Learned Ignorance: A Translation and an Appraisal of De Docta Ignorantia*. Translated by Jasper Hopkins. 2nd ed. Minneapolis: A. J. Banning, 1981.

Pepper, Stephen C. *World Hypotheses: A Study in Evidence*. Berkeley: University of California Press, 1961.

Petrarca, Francesco. *On His Own Ignorance and That of Many Others*. In *The Renaissance Philosophy of Man*, edited by Ernst Cassirer et al., 47–133. Chicago: University of Chicago Press, 1956.

Rosenkranz, Karl. *Hegels Leben*. Berlin: Duncker and Humblot, 1844.

Sandburg, Carl. *Incidentals*. Galesburg, IL: Asgard Press, 1907.

Snell, Bruno. *The Discovery of the Mind in Greek Philosophy and Literature*. Translated by T. G. Rosenmeyer. New York: Dover, 1982.

Spinoza, Benedict de. "On the Improvement of the Understanding." In vol. 2 of *The Chief Works of Benedict de Spinoza*. Translated by R. H. M. Elwes. New York: Dover, 1951.

Stace, W. T. *The Philosophy of Hegel: A Systematic Exposition*. New York: Dover, 1955.

Stirling, James Hutchison. *The Secret of Hegel: Being the Hegelian System in Origin, Principle, Form and Matter*. Edinburgh: Oliver and Boyd, 1898.

Verene, Donald Phillip. *Hegel's Recollection: A Study of Images in the Phenomenology of Spirit*. Albany: State University of New York Press, 1985.

————. *The Origins of the Philosophy of Symbolic Forms: Kant, Hegel, and Cassirer*. Evanston: Northwestern University Press, 2011.

————. *Vico's New Science: A Philosophical Commentary*. Ithaca: Cornell University Press, 2015.

Vico, Giambattista. "The Academies and the Relation between Philosophy and Eloquence." Translated by Donald Phillip Verene. In *On the Study Methods of Our Time*, translated by Elio Gianturco, 85–90. Ithaca: Cornell University Press, 1990.

————. *The Autobiography of Giambattista Vico*. Translated by Max Harold Fisch and Thomas Goddard Bergin. Ithaca: Cornell University Press, 1990.

————. "First Response." In *On the Most Ancient Wisdom of the Italians: Unearthed from the Origins of the Latin Language; Including the Disputation with the Giornale de' letterati d'Italia*, translated by L. M. Palmer, 118–35. Ithaca: Cornell University Press, 1988.

————. "On the Heroic Mind." Translated by Elizabeth Sewell and Anthony C. Sirignano. In *Vico and Contemporary Thought*, edited by Giorgio Tagliacozzo et al., 228–45. Atlantic Highlands, NJ: Humanities Press, 1979.

————. *On the Most Ancient Wisdom of the Italians: Drawn Out from the Origins of the Latin Language*. Translated by Jason Taylor. New Haven: Yale University Press, 2010.

————. *On the Study Methods of Our Time*. Translated by Elio Gianturco. Ithaca: Cornell University Press, 1990.

————. "Reprehension of the Metaphysics of René Descartes, Benedict Spinoza, and John Locke." Translated by Donald Phillip Verene. In *Giambattista Vico: Keys to the New Science; Translations, Commentaries, and Essays*, edited by Thora Ilin Bayer and Donald Phillip Verene, 179–82. Ithaca: Cornell University Press, 2009.

————. *A Translation from Latin into English of Giambattista Vico's* Il Diritto Universale/ Universal Law. Translated by John. D. Schaeffer. 2 vols. Lewiston, NY: E. Mellen, 2011.

Whitehead, Alfred North. *The Aims of Education and Other Essays*. New York: Free Press, 1967.

————. *The Function of Reason*. Boston: Beacon, 1962.

————. *Modes of Thought*. New York: Capricorn, 1958.

————. *Religion in the Making*. New York: Meridian, 1960.

————. *Science and the Modern World*. New York: Macmillan, 1925.

Ziesche, Eva. "Unbekannte Manuskripte aus der Jenaer und Nürnberger Zeit in Berliner Hegel- Nachlass." *Zeitschrift für philosophische Forschung* 29 (1975) 430–44.

Index